## ✍ **ADVANCE PRAISE** ✍

*"Mr. Monkey and Me is the truthful and oftentimes harrowing story of entrepreneurship that too often goes untold. Mike Smerklo goes through the many challenges in building ServiceSource into a successful public company, not the least of which is actually learning how to control the ever-present doubting voice inside himself."*

—SCOTT KUPOR, MANAGING PARTNER OF ANDREESSEN
HOROWITZ, AUTHOR OF *SECRETS OF SAND HILL
ROAD: VENTURE CAPITAL AND HOW TO GET IT*

*"A perfect encapsulation of the negative inner dialogue we have with ourselves and how to manage it."*

—LYNN JURICH, CEO AND CO-FOUNDER OF SUNRUN

*"By conquering self-doubt and using it to fuel your passion and attain your goals, Mr. Monkey and Me provides a thoughtful and provocative perspective on the entrepreneurial journey. This book is truly unique thanks to Mike's humor, mindset, and expertise."*

—IRV GROUSBECK, ADJUNCT PROFESSOR OF MANAGEMENT AT
STANFORD GRADUATE SCHOOL OF BUSINESS, CO-FOUNDER,
STANFORD CENTER FOR ENTREPRENEURIAL STUDIES

"*Aspiring entrepreneurs, this book is a must read. It takes more than a brilliant idea and venture funding to make it as an entrepreneur, and in this book, Mike gives it to us straight. Mike shares his earned wisdom with humility, deep intelligence, and the comedy that makes this book such a thought-provoking and enjoyable read.*"

—JESSICA HERRIN, CEO AND FOUNDER OF STELLA & DOT, AUTHOR OF *FIND YOUR EXTRAORDINARY: DREAM BIGGER, LIVE HAPPIER, AND ACHIEVE SUCCESS ON YOUR OWN TERMS*

"*I've known Mike for almost two decades, both as an entrepreneur and more recently as an investor, and he's got a unique set of experiences upon which to base the wisdom of Mr. Monkey and Me. Anyone in the startup world can learn a lot from Mike!*"

—BRUCE DUNLEVIE, FOUNDER AND GENERAL PARTNER OF BENCHMARK

"*Perhaps the toughest challenge of entrepreneurship has nothing to do with raising capital, scaling, or talent management—instead it's an ongoing battle between your ears with voices of doubt often ruling the day. In his new book, Mike Smerklo pulls back the curtain and gives an inside view on the battle so many face but rarely discuss—mental health.*"

—DIANE TAVENNER, CO-FOUNDER AND CEO OF SUMMIT PUBLIC SCHOOLS, AUTHOR OF *PREPARED: WHAT KIDS NEED FOR A FULFILLED LIFE*

*"Mr. Monkey and Me gives a no-nonsense approach to entrepreneurship providing actionable and honest insight. Something most traditional business books don't do!"*

*"Mike Smerklo speaks to the heart of everyone who's been mulling that great business idea for years but just doesn't have the courage to start. He tackles the challenges that come with taking the plunge in his part-memoir-part-survival guide, Mr. Monkey and Me. This book is for anyone on the edge of the diving board, wanting to dive into entrepreneurship but just needs one final push."*

*"Mr. Monkey and Me is the perfect read for everyone who wants to know what running a business actually looks like before the million dollar company comes to fruition. Mike doesn't serve to discourage anyone from entering startup life; rather, he encourages his readers to take the risk and gives them all the right tools to succeed."*

*"The world desperately needs more entrepreneurs. Mike Smerklo writes an important, deeply personal and quite entertaining book about one of the biggest challenges in being an entrepreneur—managing your psyche along the very challenging but often rewarding entrepreneurial path. I wish I'd been able to read this twenty years ago!"*

"Mike Smerklo has lived every facet of the 'real' entrepreneur life. Bootstrapped. Venture-backed. Hyper-growth. IPO. It's extremely rare to find this frontline expertise in one entrepreneur—and even rarer to find it in a single book. I highly recommend Mr. Monkey and Me to any entrepreneur, whether first-time founder or seasoned innovator. This book delivers candor, insights, inspiration, and results."

—JASON DORSEY, MULTIPLE COMPANY FOUNDER AND AUTHOR OF *ZCONOMY: HOW GEN Z WILL CHANGE THE FUTURE OF BUSINESS—AND WHAT TO DO ABOUT IT*

"The world needs entrepreneurs now more than ever to solve society's many challenges, but the standard advice on entrepreneurship completely misses the most fundamental tool required: the right mindset and the ability to persevere. In Mr. Monkey and Me, Smerklo delivers a no-nonsense, no buzzword look at what it is really like to be a startup founder. This is raw, real, and spoken-from-the-heart advice, and this is a must read for anyone daring enough to be a creative founder today."

—JON CALLAGHAN, FOUNDER AND MANAGING PARTNER OF TRUE VENTURES

"Mike weaves a spellbinding story that is sure to encourage the inner entrepreneur in all of us. I love the rare look into the hard scrabble upbringing of a man who has since triumphed in the business world; Smerklo inspires us all."

—BRIAN SPALY, CHAIRMAN OF TECOVAS, FOUNDER AND CEO OF TRUNK CLUB

"In Mr. Monkey and Me, Mike has laid out everything no one tells you about starting a business. Not only has he given clear, cliche-free guidance, but it's an engaging read you won't want to put down. I can't recommend this book enough to anyone interested in entrepreneurship."

—DAVID KENNEDY, FOUNDER AND PARTNER OF SERENT CAPITAL

"There isn't a day that I don't think about the great things Mike did as a CEO, along with the 'not great.' I am extremely grateful for the lessons Mike taught me—and so excited that with Mr. Monkey and Me, he is bringing these lessons to a wider audience."

—JAY ACKERMAN, PRESIDENT AND CEO OF REVELEER

"Mike keeps his readers grounded in reality in this practical and entertaining guide to the ups and downs of his own entrepreneurial journey, Mr. Monkey and Me. He shows young entrepreneurs a path to success that might look less glamorous than what you see on TV, but one that is well worn and time-tested by the most successful innovators in business."

—BRIAN SHARPLES, CO-FOUNDER AND CEO OF HOMEAWAY

"Mike hit the nail on the head with this one—all entrepreneurs should read Mr. Monkey and Me and share with a mentee. Powerful perspective and advice!"

—JIM ELLIS, CO-FOUNDER OF ASURION, LECTURER IN MANAGEMENT AT THE GRADUATE SCHOOL OF BUSINESS AT STANFORD UNIVERSITY

*"Any entrepreneur suffering from imposter syndrome needs to read Mr. Monkey and Me. Mike walks readers through what it's like to move from a leader who feels like they are a "play actor," trying to lead by imagining what other, more successful CEOs would do, to authentically pursuing the vision and direction that they think is best for an organization. Mike takes on the stereotype alpha male CEO and proves why all personalities have the potential to be great leaders."*

—NIRAV TOLIA, CO-FOUNDER AND FORMER CHIEF
EXECUTIVE OFFICER OF NEXTDOOR

*"Mike makes entrepreneurship tangible, exciting, and fulfilling without the usual cliches. Mr. Monkey and Me isn't about simply flaunting his (very considerable) success, it's also about vulnerability and sacrifice, preparing his audience for a unique approach to balancing life and work—and steeling it against that occasional little voice inside that says, 'You'll never make it.'"*

—WILLIAM N. THORNDIKE, JR., MANAGING GENERAL PARTNER
OF HOUSATONIC PARTNERS, AUTHOR OF *THE OUTSIDERS*

*"Mr. Monkey and Me feels more like a casual conversation with your successful buddy than a guide to entrepreneurial success. Mike is equal parts hilarious, genuine, and informative in his one-of-a-kind book. He shares his personal successes and failures to help the next generation of founders develop the mental fortitude needed to achieve their dreams."*

—MARK LESLIE, CO-FOUNDER, CHAIRMAN AND CEO OF VERITAS
SOFTWARE, MANAGING GENERAL PARTNER OF LESLIE VENTURES

"Do you listen to someone who has watched a little golf on TV or someone who has won on the PGA? Mike took a business from nothing to a multibillion dollar public company. He not only walks you through his amazing journey, but he also does it in the most honest and open way. And you will never forget Mr. Monkey."

—COTTER CUNNINGHAM, FOUNDER AND CEO OF RETAILMENOT

"Mike's authenticity around the trials and tribulations of entrepreneurship are unrivaled. He speaks from the head, heart, and soul, and his story and counsel will inspire the next generation of leaders."

—JOHN PLEASANTS, CO-FOUNDER AND CEO OF BRAVA

"Part coach, part shrink, part colleague, Smerklo takes you down an entertaining journey of work and life, leaving you laughing and cringing...and better suited to lead an organization."

—DAVID DODSON, STANFORD GRADUATE SCHOOL OF BUSINESS

"All entrepreneurs face countless gut-wrenching life and business decisions. I was fortunate to have Mike Smerklo in my corner to generously share his battle scars, sense of humor, and hard-earned wisdom. This book is classic Mike: thoughtful, vulnerable, really funny, and dead right."

—BILL CLERICO, CO-FOUNDER AND CEO OF WEPAY

"Mike Smerklo knows that all entrepreneurs need to get comfortable being uncomfortable. Mr. Monkey and Me explores Smerklo navigating playing the tough leader, the empathetic boss, the risk taker and the guy that always gets it right. After many successes and many failures, Smerklo learned that the correct way to lead is really somewhere in the balance of all those different roles. He teaches how to get comfortable with tension and find a way forward."

—NEAL DEMPSEY, MANAGING GENERAL PARTNER OF BAY PARTNERS, ONE OF THE LONGEST-RUNNING VENTURE CAPITAL FIRMS IN SILICON VALLEY, AND LECTURER AT THE UNIVERSITY OF WASHINGTON'S FOSTER SCHOOL OF BUSINESS

"Mr. Monkey and Me offers a wonderfully refreshing combination of honesty and great storytelling that makes it a must for every entrepreneur's bookshelf—or at least those entrepreneurs interested in the harsh reality of it all."

—BRIAN CRUVER, SERIAL ENTREPRENEUR AND FOUNDER AND CEO OF ALERT MEDIA

"The Monkey and Me is an essential read for any current or aspiring entrepreneur. At a time when we need entrepreneurs more than ever to solve great challenges and create jobs, Smerklo offers invaluable insights on the mental tenacity needed to build a successful business."

—BRYNNE KENNEDY, FOUNDER OF TOPIA, AUTHOR OF FLAT, FLUID AND FAST, AND A CALIFORNIA CONGRESSIONAL CANDIDATE

*"An honest review of the entrepreneur life that will make anyone who's been questioning if it's the right time to start their own business feel confident, informed, and excited."*

—CLINT GREENLEAF, CEO OF CONTENT CAPITAL

*"I've never had a name for that negative voice in my head, but now I do! Nice to meet you, Mr. Monkey."*

—BILL EGAN, FOUNDER AND GENERAL PARTNER OF
BURR, EGAN, DELEAGE & CO. AND MARION EQUITY
PARTNERS, FORMER PARTNER OF TA ASSOCIATES

*"Growing up broke in Toledo, Mike Smerklo has gone on to achieve success few could imagine. Now he's written a book that tells us how he did it and how we could as well. Authentic, practical, inspiring, and actionable. One of the best books on entrepreneurship I've ever read."*

—MICHAEL FITZGERALD, CO-FOUNDER AND CEO OF SUBMITTABLE

*"Mike Smerklo delivers pithy and personal lessons in Mr. Monkey and Me. His riveting experience with both gut-punch setbacks and exhilarating successes makes for an entertaining read. Full of effective tools for young business owners to fine tune their mental approach, this entertaining book provides unusual and useful wisdom for leading entrepreneurial growth."*

—PETER KELLY, LECTURER IN MANAGEMENT AT
STANFORD GRADUATE SCHOOL OF BUSINESS

"In Mr. Monkey and Me, Mike Smerklo takes a different look at the entrepreneurial process, examining the not often discussed voices of doubt that plague us all and stop many would-be entrepreneurs before realizing their dreams and making their much-needed impact on the world. Believing the world needs all the innovative ideas and entrepreneurs it can get right now, Smerklo uses his own unlikely and challenged upbringing as the backdrop to elucidate his own entrepreneurial journey, showing where and how these voices grow within us, often armed with a more powerful punch than outside forces to derail our efforts. Smerklo then smartly outlines actionable tools he used to cut off their oxygen and persevere. Mike believes anyone can have the entrepreneurial spirit; they just need to recognize it and know how to beat the monkey standing in their way."

—SHAWN K. O'NEILL, MANAGING DIRECTOR OF
SILVER LAKE, GROUP HEAD OF SLW


"Mike is a long-time mentor and friend, and reading Mr. Monkey and Me reminded me of the many lessons he taught me and not-so-gentle nudges he gave me over the years. Mr. Monkey and Me is a refresher course in what it truly takes to succeed as an entrepreneur and is a no BS account of a remarkable entrepreneurial journey. It shines a light on the hardest part of being a successful entrepreneur: mastering your own fears and shortcomings. I recommend it for anyone entering the fray!"

—NATALIE MCCULLOUGH, PRESIDENT AND
COO OF DOMINO DATA LAB

*"An entertaining roadmap to conquer your self-doubt and work with authenticity toward your entrepreneurial journey."*

—GERALD RISK, ENTREPRENEUR, INVESTOR, AND LECTURER IN MANAGEMENT AT STANFORD UNIVERSITY GRADUATE SCHOOL OF BUSINESS

*"Mike Smerklo deeply understands the challenges and triumphs of being an entrepreneur. Mike applies his experience to help entrepreneurs handle perhaps the toughest challenge of entrepreneurship—wrestling with the voices between your own ears. Honest and vulnerable, Mr. Monkey and Me is a gift to current and future entrepreneurs."*

—DOUG TOMLINSON, FOUNDER AND CEO OF VINO VOLO

*"Hilarious tone with serious takeaways. What better way to tell a story about entrepreneurship."*

—BARRY REYNOLDS, MANAGING DIRECTOR OF HOUSATONIC PARTNERS

*"In Mr. Monkey and Me, Mike Smerklo names that little voice we all have in our head. All entrepreneurs struggle with self doubt. Smerklo teaches his readers not to avoid the monkey but how to confront and quiet it, and succeed in spite of it."*

—SARAH PUIL, FOUNDER AND CEO OF BOXT

"Choosing to be an entrepreneur is one of the most rewarding—and challenging—career paths anyone can take. Maintaining the emotional fortitude necessary to weather the inevitable ups and downs is critical but not something taught at business schools or in management books. With great candor, humility, and humor, Mike Smerklo shares lessons from his own entrepreneurial journey and the tools he's developed to get the odds on your side. Smerklo's SHAPE framework is a comprehensive and actionable model for staying on track and keeping Mr. Monkey at bay. With Mr. Monkey and Me, Smerklo has created an invaluable resource for anyone courageous enough to take the entrepreneurial leap."

—PETER GIFFORD, PRESIDENT AND PARTNER
OF REGIS MANAGEMENT COMPANY, LLC

"Mike cuts right to the chase in Mr. Monkey and Me. His riveting experience with the ups and downs of entrepreneurship teaches young business owners how to fine tune their mental prowess for the journey ahead and come out on top!"

—NICK MEHTA, CEO OF GAININSIGHT

"Mr. Monkey and Me puts an emphasis on mental fortitude needed in entrepreneurship—not as an afterthought but a foundation for success."

—MATT ROSENBERG, CHIEF REVENUE OFFICER AT COMPASS

*"Mike Smerklo redefines what it means to be an entrepreneur in Mr. Monkey and Me. Reflecting on his experience scaling a small business into a publicly traded company worth nearly a billion dollars in value, Smerklo wants his readers to know that being a true entrepreneur means knowing they're going to make a bunch of mistakes, and need to be more than just 'okay' with it. It's only lonely at the top if you're too afraid to ask for help."*

—ZEYNEP YOUNG, CEO AT CALYTERA

# MR. MONKEY AND ME

A REAL Survival Guide for Entrepreneurs

MR. MONKEY AND ME

MIKE SMERKLO

**LIONCREST**
PUBLISHING

MR. MONKEY AND ME

*A Real Survival Guide for Entrepreneurs*

ISBN   978-1-5445-1498-7 *Hardcover*

978-1-5445-1496-3 *Paperback*

978-1-5445-1724-7 *Ebook*

*This book is dedicated to all the entrepreneurs in the world—those brave enough to bring an idea into an indifferent world and give it their all in the hopes of turning a dream into reality.*

*Thank you for getting into the arena to fight the fight. You are an inspiration to all of us.*

# CONTENTS

# AUTHOR'S NOTE

The events in this book are as I remember them. I tried my best to avoid any inaccuracies in stories, but details have never been my strong suit. If errors appear, they are the result of the passage of time, my advancing age, or some coping mechanism. Or a combination of all three. While I have taken some literary license with the dialogue, I believe the content provided accurately depicts the spirit of the moment. However, I have changed a few names out of respect for privacy or because I was unable to contact the person in the story.

For those reading this who worked directly or indirectly for me: I only now realize what a complete asshole I was during my time as an entrepreneur. I am sincerely sorry. It's a lame excuse, but as every charlatan, stripper, or prostitute has said throughout the history of time, "I was young, and I needed the money."

# INTRODUCTION

*"Life is either a daring adventure or nothing."*

—HELEN KELLER

Before you dive into this book, let me tell you what it *isn't*.

The usual shit.

You know what I'm talking about—the books that line the business section of any major bookstore, the stuff that comes up when you search "entrepreneur" on Amazon, and the books other people recommend as the roadmaps to starting a business.

There's also an endless stream of articles equivalent to entrepreneurial junk food that does little to help. I'm sure you've read this bullshit from time to time; short blog posts like, *The Ten Things Elon Musk Does Before Breakfast Every*

*Morning*, or *How to Streamline Your Wardrobe Like Mark Zuckerberg*. Reading these articles is like eating an entire bag of Doritos when you're starving. It's good going down, but you feel pretty gross afterwards, and you haven't consumed anything of substance.

I don't have anything to say about the "usual shit" that hasn't already been said. Trust me, that information is out there. I'm not interested in rehashing it or putting my personal spin on it.

I'm *far* more interested in what I call "the other shit."

If you're embarking on an entrepreneurial journey, you want to create a great company. That is table stakes. But how do you develop the mental tenacity to make your dream a reality?

Maybe you've hit some stumbling blocks with your business. Maybe you're not sure how to get started. Maybe you're wrestling with the voice of self-doubt (I've named my own inner voice of self-doubt Mr. Monkey, and he's really the star of this book).

When I started out, I read all the usual shit. It got me 80 percent of the way there, but it couldn't answer the deeper questions I had about what makes a great *entrepreneur*, not just a great *business*.

What was the mental game, and how could I win it? What was between the ears of the great entrepreneurs I most admired, and how could I learn from what they'd learned? How could I practice and build the level of mental toughness I knew I was going to need if I was going to swim, not sink?

When I went looking for *that* kind of guidance, I couldn't find much of it. The truth is, the "other shit" doesn't get taught in business schools, and it rarely gets written about. It's the kind of knowledge that only comes from building a business with sweat, tears, and the hardest work of your life. Don't get me wrong; strategy, industry, competition, timing, resources, and all the rest are incredibly important. But all those factors being equal, the difference between success and failure in business is *mindset*.

That's why I wrote this book. I wrote it for all the entrepreneurs out there starting out, or wondering why they're struggling—all of you looking for the other shit. Now more than ever, the world needs entrepreneurship. The world needs *you*.

## THE WORLD NEEDS ENTREPRENEURS—LIKE YOU

If you've picked up this book, my guess is that you have ideas, passion, and a desire to pave your own way as an entrepreneur. You want to build something. The world needs entrepreneurs like you, and I am glad you are reading this book. The major breakthroughs in the world happen via innovation and entrepreneurship. The collective wisdom of governments, large organizations, and not-for-profit organizations certainly contribute to the advancement of the human race, but I would rather bet on entrepreneurs to solve the major issues facing us today than any of the aforementioned entities.

Simply put, we need more entrepreneurs building solutions to tough problems. However, for a lot of potential entrepreneurs, the path forward is hard to imagine. It certainly was for me. I grew up in a low-income family in the Rust Belt of the United States. I struggled to visualize a path forward, and my role models—as you will see later on in this book—were not exactly inspirational characters. However, I humbly recognize that I am a white male who grew up in the United States in a time of relative peace and prosperity. It wasn't simple, but comparatively speaking, I had it easier than most.

The lack of diversity in entrepreneurship is real. In 2018, less than 3 percent of the $85 *billion* invested in venture capital dollars went to women and minorities. This is a complicated cycle and well beyond the scope of this book. I don't have all the answers. But I do know that entrepreneurship is critical to many aspects of our society by changing lives and communities, and creating jobs and wealth.

So how do we get more potential entrepreneurs to raise their hands and get started? What are the mental roadblocks that typically get in the way? How do we get more talented people working on real problems, big or small? How can successful entrepreneurs stay on track and avoid the "dumb shit" that trips them up?

I believe that the opportunity of entrepreneurship can only start when someone has the confidence to begin the journey. To raise their hand, so to speak, and say "I want to give it a shot." The goal of this book is to help you find the courage to raise your hand, see the opportunities in front of you and pursue your dreams.

I want you to approach entrepreneurship wisely and with the support of a formula that can help you survive and thrive as an entrepreneur. I am going to tell you a lot of stories in this book, and I hope you enjoy them. I also hope they help you relate. You're not the only one who's stumbled in the process of building entrepreneurial success. I believe your dream is important, and I want to help you make it happen.

## WHY I WROTE THIS BOOK (AND WHAT'S IN IT FOR YOU)

I was the first person in my immediate family to go to college. To afford the cost of state school tuition, I worked three jobs during the school year and another two most summers. I graduated with a degree in accounting from Miami University in Oxford, Ohio, and moved to Chicago to start my career as a CPA. My first job paid me a whopping $27,000 a year, which immediately made me the highest-earning member in Smerklo family history. How exciting!

I spent my early career in jobs that taught me business fundamentals, but I hated those jobs—they drained my soul. I extended my education with an MBA and finally started my entrepreneurial journey right after 9/11. I took an unusual path to entrepreneurship, buying a small business and then running it for more than a decade. I experienced all of the highs and lows that go with being an entrepreneur. I screwed up so many times I lost count and damn near went crazy along the way.

I loved being an entrepreneur. It's the best job in the world... but *damn*, it was hard. So fucking hard.

These days, I spend my time helping other entrepreneurs reach their dreams by investing in startups across the United States through the venture capital firm I co-founded in 2015, Next Coast Ventures. Now, I am able to provide money and expertise to the next generation of entrepreneurs, which allows me to help them in the ways so many people helped me along my path. At the point of writing this book, Next Coast Ventures has raised two venture capital funds and invested in over forty companies, deploying several hundred million dollars in capital to help startups grow. Each year, I meet with nearly a thousand startups in the hope of finding one or two founders to back. This provides me with another lens into what successful entrepreneurs do—and don't do—to remain mentally strong throughout the rollercoaster ride that is running a business.

This book will delve into the mindset required for successful entrepreneurship: ways to cope, how to build mental toughness, and specific work-life lessons that can only come from someone who has been through it all. The real story is one of grit. The rollercoaster highs are thrilling, but the gutwrenching lows have damn near killed just about anyone who has tried their hand at starting and running a business.

The sobering truth is that most startups fail. Skip over this incredibly important fact, and we'd be doing an injustice to the courage it takes to step into the entrepreneurial arena.

I'm not here to discourage you, though.

From my perspective, both as an entrepreneur and from watching amazing leaders build tremendous companies, I can tell you that there is no better job in the world than starting, running, and growing a business. It takes time, sacrifice, and hard work to develop a solid idea that customers will be willing to pay for and set up the infrastructure to support it. Most importantly, successful entrepreneurship takes a level of mental strength that cannot be understated.

It might be the number one differentiator between success and failure.

But the mental aspect of entrepreneurship rarely, if ever, gets talked about. When it does, it's typically a passing mention of "self-care," as if it were an afterthought of the journey. This book brings the mental aspect of entrepreneurship front and center to help you build the mental fitness you need to really be successful.

Of course, mental fitness alone will never be a substitute for a good business model, solid strategy, and access to resources such as capital and talent. Without these ingredients, your idea will likely never get off the ground. However, all other elements being equal, the right mental mindset can be the difference between success and failure.

In the chapters that follow, I am going to tell you all the shit they don't teach you in business school. We'll talk about mental toughness, how to manage self-doubt, how to ask for help, and how to find a real-world work-life balance (or cope when you can't).

Through my experiences as an entrepreneur and now as a venture capitalist, I developed the SHAPE Mindset. It'll help you take care of yourself and grow your abilities by exploring these key areas:

**S**elf—As in know thyself

**H**elp—How and when to find the support you need

**A**uthenticity—Make decisions based on who you are as a leader

**P**ersistence—Keep after it, even if it seems impossible

**E**xpectations—Set your sights on the right goals to maximize your success

The goal is to provide you with some context and specific, actionable steps to help you get out of the shower, dry off, put some clothes on, and get after your entrepreneurial dream. At the end of each chapter, you will find what I call "monkey minders," or clear actionable steps, to help you make it happen.

One final note before we dive in: I want to be clear about what this book is *not*.

This book is not a victory lap, and it's not a memoir. I'd place my career somewhere in the "good, not great" category—like a solid B-list actor in Hollywood. I've done fine, but let's save the memoir bookshelf space for the A-list entrepreneurs.

In my time as an entrepreneur, I screwed up just about every aspect of the SHAPE formula. I could fill countless pages with my failures and the endless struggles I encountered with my own personal demons. But something tells me that sharing stories of excessive drinking, explosive temper tantrums, and suicidal thoughts won't necessarily help you "get out of the shower and get after it."

The mindset formula you'll learn *really* comes from wisdom I gained from a broad spectrum of entrepreneurs *much* more successful than me. The SHAPE formula includes the best practices I've compiled from the extraordinary leaders, mentors, and entrepreneurs who have shaped my life.

I *am* going to share some stories from my life, but these are really to help you relate. I hope they make you laugh (or cringe) as you get to know to my inner voice of self-doubt— Mr. Monkey—and come to recognize his debilitating power. The goal of the SHAPE formula is to help you neutralize your own Mr. or Mrs. Monkey as best you can. I haven't learned to make him go away entirely, but I *have* learned to quiet him, even if just for a short time. I want to help you do the same.

I am here to help you through your entrepreneurial journey. I want you to make the third of your life you spend working intentional and meaningful. I want you to know that you are not alone. It might feel like you are, and maybe you don't think you are worthy of giving business a try. Trust me, I know the feeling—it's the number one reason I wrote this book. It is time to get out of the shower, dry off, and get ready to make it happen. It's time to raise your hand.

# CHAPTER ONE

# I COULD HAVE BEEN A SERIAL KILLER

*A census taker once tried to test me. I ate his liver with some fava beans and a nice Chianti.*

—DR. HANNIBAL LECTER, *SILENCE OF THE LAMBS*

My wife likes to joke that, given my childhood, it would be perfectly understandable if I had grown up to be a legendary serial killer. That it would make sense for me to be locked up in a maximum security prison right now, biding my time in a cold, dark cell instead of writing this book.

I prefer to say that, given where I came from, I wasn't supposed to end up where I did.

I grew up in Toledo, Ohio, in the shadow of the Standard Oil Refinery, where the air smelled like burning oil, and everyone around me seemed to be spinning their wheels. Alcoholism, divorce, and debt were the themes of my early childhood. Positive role models, if any, came from television sitcoms, but the lives we saw on TV seemed so far removed from our own, that even realistic scenarios played out like high fantasy. My family members chased their laughter at the characters on the screen with color commentary like, "Yeah, right," or "Must be nice."

I was raised by a single mom who worked her ass off as a dental hygienist. My deadbeat dad didn't pay child support and was absent from my life. Eventually, my mother remarried. My stepfather Dave had his heart in the right place but could best be described as a loveable loser. Everyone liked Dave—and everyone took advantage of him. He was six-foot-two and gangly, with a mustache and a mess of curly hair, and he liked nothing better than to tell corny jokes.

"Hey, Mike," he'd call out. "What did Kenny Rogers say when the tire fell off the back of his car?"

"What?" I'd ask to humor him.

"You picked a fine time to leave me, loose wheel." *Groan.*

Dave sold auto-repair tools to mechanics, drove an enormous ugly yellow Mac Tool truck, and filled our garage with inventory. My mom's second job was trying to help him run his business. He came home every night and gave her the sales reports for the day.

I can still picture him in his Mac shirt, covered in grease because he hadn't showered yet. He'd sit there scratching his head while my mom went over the numbers. When she finished, she'd slump over, defeated.

"How could you have sold so little?" she'd say. "If we don't sell more, we'll never be able to pay off the inventory."

It was like *Death of a Salesman* happening in real time, with my stepfather starring as Willie Loman. Watching them try to run this small business without any skills or resources made my stomach churn with anxiety.

*You don't have a boss. You make your own hours. No one tells you what to do. You choose where and when you want to work.* Those are the fantasies people have of entrepreneurship when they're sitting in the corporate cubicle on a beautiful day wishing they could play a round of golf. My stepfather technically had all that freedom, but because he was not mentally prepared to be an entrepreneur, he got the worst of business ownership. There was no safety net. No escape. Dave would have been better off getting a corporate job with regular income, so he could come home at five o'clock in the evening, knowing he was done for the day.

Dave and my mom worked eighty hours a week to make $23,000 a year and never took a vacation. Church on Sunday counted as a break. They were always on the edge of going broke. It felt as if the harder my mom and Dave worked, the faster they sank.

This was my first exposure to entrepreneurship, and I didn't think I wanted any part of it. It was terrifying to watch. "Luckily," I had other adult role models to provide perspective, like my dear old grandmother.

## PEOPLE IN HELL...

I was eight years old, spending the night at my grandmother's, which was one of my least favorite things to do. She wasn't the warm, fuzzy kind of grandma who bakes cookies and lets you get away with everything. My grandmother was uncomfortable in her own skin and angry with her fate in life. She smoked constantly and taught me how to mix drinks so I could make myself useful and keep her glass full.

While getting ice to make my grandmother the first Manhattan of my visit, I noticed a box of Push-Ups ice cream pops in the freezer. I wanted one, but she usually got angry when I asked for things. I had to think strategically. If she had enough to drink, she'd get sleepy, and that would be my best shot.

I waited patiently while she spewed racist rantings about

Jews and Mexicans and the us-versus-them mentality that shaped her worldview as though she were being interviewed on CNN and someone had asked to her to share her very important opinions. I daydreamed about that ice cream in the freezer while she lit up another Virginia Slim and slipped into a drunken stupor.

Eventually, she sent me in to make her a "nightcap," which is what she called her last drink of the evening. I mixed the drink, rehearsing my question over and over in my mind, building up my confidence. But when I brought the glass out to her, the words felt scrambled in my brain. I started to stammer.

"Uh, Grandma?"

"What?"

"Um, I—I saw some ice cream in the freezer."

"So?" she said, lit up by the question. "What are you getting at?" She had to have known what I wanted, but she wasn't going to make it easy for me. She would force me to ask.

Finally, I mustered the courage and said, "Could I have some ice cream?"

"You want some ice cream?"

"Yeah, Grandma, I would really love some ice cream."

She took her drink from my hand, slammed it in a few gulps, and stood up to go inside. As she opened the screen door, she turned back to me.

"Well," she said, "People in hell want ice water."

I stood on the patio listening to her laugh hysterically all the way to her bedroom. The night was over, and I wasn't getting ice cream.

What she was telling me was the core of her belief system, a discouraging hymn against hopes and dreams that she was certain would only lead to disappointment:

> *Life's tough. Suck it up. Don't think you're better than us. Don't think you deserve more. You're stuck in Toledo, Ohio, kid. Blame, escape, and get through life. We don't get what we want. It's futile. The sooner you accept this, the better off you'll be.*

This mantra took up residence in my young brain like a blaring radio alarm I couldn't turn off. I didn't want to believe it, but most of my family reinforced the message throughout my formative years. Some days the message came across louder than others—like on "relaxing" summer Sunday afternoons.

## SUNDAY "FUN DAY"

When I was in my pre-teens, we had an aboveground pool. Every Sunday while the weather was warm, my extended family would gather on the deck after church. I'd splash around with my cousins while the adults played Trivial Pursuit and drank their way to a Monday morning hangover.

At some point in the day, my Uncle Joe would ride over on his motorcycle to join Sunday Fun Day. In between wives at this time (number two long gone, number three not yet in the picture), Uncle Joe would pull into the gravel driveway, his latest girlfriend clinging to his back, and his trusty Styrofoam cooler filled with eighteen Miller Lites strapped to the luggage rack. Then he'd hop off his Harley, climb the stairs, pop open the first beer of the day, and immediately begin what he called his Indian Sun Dance.

"Hiya, hiya, hiya, ho!" he would yell out, bringing his hand to his mouth, athletic shorts and spread collar golf shirt flapping as he spun in a circle, magically not spilling his beer. Sunday Fun Day had officially begun, Uncle Joe style.

One of those Sunday Fun Days had a meaningful impact in my life, despite the relative insignificance at the time. As usual, once Uncle Joe had gotten about six or eight beers in him, he wanted to play some football. This meant grabbing me and my cousin Jon and making us run football plays. At first, we kind of liked it; it was something fun to do on a hot day when nothing else was going on. But soon, Uncle Joe would have a few more beers and get too serious about the game.

Uncle Joe would turn into Uncle Rico, from *Napoleon Dynamite* fame, right before our eyes.

"Okay, Mike, the defense is getting soft," Uncle Joe said as if gathering an entire team together to run a two-minute drill in hopes of winning the Super Bowl. "Jon's getting a little tired. I think if you do a ten-yard fade route to the sidelines, we'll be able to beat him." He was dead serious.

I remember looking at him thinking, *We're in a small patch of grass. The sideline is the neighbors' single-story house. The fade route entails me running around the compost pile. Plus, there's only two of us playing, and Jon can hear what you're saying.* But it seemed important to him, so I agreed.

"All right, right, right," Uncle Joe shouted. "Get up to the line! Blue 47! Blue 47! Set, hut, hut, hike!"

I ran down ten yards to precisely where he told me. Joe rifled the football at me, but I didn't get my hands up fast enough. *Boom!* The ball hit me right in the chest, knocking me over. The sting hurt like hell, but the worst part was, I knew I couldn't cry. Absolutely not. Under no circumstances could I cry in front of Uncle Joe.

My cousin Jon picked me up and said, "This is stupid, Mike; don't worry about it."

But as soon as I turned around, I saw the look in Uncle Joe's eyes.

"Goddammit, Mike!" Joe screamed. "You've got to get ready. Get after it! This is not a drill! You've got to DO something! Don't be a pussy!"

Back in the pool, I tried to shake it off. There was a big red welt on my chest where the football hit. The look of disdain on his face when he screamed at me had shaken me to my core.

Overall, even though Uncle Joe could be hard on me, he wasn't a bad guy, just a little crazy. I was being raised by a single mom, and he was the most important male figure in my life. I think he realized that and took the responsibility to heart. He was a product of his time and a certain kind of hyper-masculine energy, but he did care about me. Whenever he did explode at me, it was always the same message:

*You better get after it, man. Don't be soft. Suck it up. You better work your ass off to get out of here.*

*I think what he was really saying was: Don't let yourself get stuck being me.*

Or, at least, I'd love to think that's what it was.

Because of all his shouting, Uncle Joe became a loud contributor to my inner voice, and while some of it was painful, some of it was motivating. He was trying to give me a call to action, of sorts, but the emphasis was always on toughness, on being a man, although his idea of what a man was supposed to be was ill-defined. Though it was shallow and limited in view, the way I internalized Uncle Joe's voice did encourage me toward hard work and effort in some strange way. *Goddammit, I have to succeed. I have to do something to get out of here. Don't be weak. Whatever you do, don't be weak.*

It was as if he'd grabbed me and said, "Don't let this be your destiny."

He never actually said that. It would've probably been more helpful. But I'll give Joe the benefit of the doubt and believe that's what he was trying to tell me.

## GET A LIFE...OR AT LEAST A GREAT MATTRESS

Since my stepdad Dave had more heart than common sense, he'd often sell a toolbox to a mechanic and take a used car in trade if they didn't have the money to pay. As a result, our driveway looked like a used car lot. The only upside was that I got to drive one of those piece-of-shit cars to school.

As a senior in high school, my "car of the year" was a 1974 Oldsmobile Cutlass Supreme (faded cherry red, thank you very much). One gray January morning, I was up early for basketball practice, driving to school in the rain. I was senior class president, captain of the basketball team, and hoping that if I could put together an excellent basketball season, I might get a scholarship to college. Perhaps I could get out of Toledo, get a degree, and maybe start a business that didn't require an overflow of tools in a garage. I didn't know what I wanted beyond that. I just knew that I didn't want the life that would be ahead of me if I stayed.

I fiddled with the FM radio, trying to find something to take my mind off the dreariness of the day.

"Every day. Every day!" a booming voice shouted from the tinny speakers. I was about to change the station, but something about the voice made me pause.

"Every day of your life, you spend one-third of your time sleeping. So why don't you have a great mattress?"

Although it was just some gimmicky local radio commercial, it hit me in a profound way. My mind got stuck on this simple question: If a third of your life is spent sleeping, *what are the other two-thirds spent doing?*

I thought about my mom and stepdad pouring their time into

running that struggling auto-tool business. I thought of my grandma and her "worldviews" and of Uncle Joe, desperately living his miserable week just for Sunday Fun Day. They all did the same thing every day, *every day.* That was what their other two-thirds looked like.

I shut off the radio and drove in silence, thinking. It was the first time I'd stopped to wonder, *what am I going to do with my life?* If a third of life is spent sleeping, a third of it is potentially spent with friends and family, then a third of your life is spent at your job. I didn't know what I wanted to do. Still, I knew for certain that I didn't want to end up like any of my adult "role models," feeling like every part of life was insurmountable.

On that soggy drive to school, I vowed that I was not going to live my life the way I saw everyone around me living. And while I had absolutely no idea what to do about this painfully strong emotion or where it would take me, I knew there had to be a different path.

## GETTING OUT OF TOLEDO

This is the point in most business books where I tell you I had a brilliant idea, used my amazing intellect to build an empire, and became a billionaire seemingly overnight. That's how the script goes, right?

Not this one. All I knew at the time was that I wanted something different from what I saw around me. My goal was simply to get out of Toledo. The only problem? I had no idea how.

I couldn't ask anyone in our inner circle, "How did you get out?" because no one ever did. Everyone around me was poor. We were all stuck in the same rigged game. The adults around me were all doing the best they could with the limited perspective and education available to them, but it was never enough. No one knew how to get ahead. That's what Toledo symbolized for me: it wasn't just geography, it was a mindset of failure, of being trapped.

Until I went away to college, I had never seen anyone who achieved any notable level of success. I had no map for how to construct a different life. So instead, I took the idea of what I *didn't* want to be and focused on how to move in a different direction.

My mom didn't know exactly how to coach me either. The only advice she gave me—over and over—was simple. "Get educated," she implored me. "Please Mike, just go to college." Every day, I say a prayer of thanks to her for that simple push. Modest goals and small steps is how all journeys start, right?

I would go to college. I would leave Toledo. And I did—I got out.

## MY JOURNEY OUT

I graduated in 1991 from Miami University with a degree in accounting, working part-time throughout my entire four years to help pay for the in-state tuition. I moved to Chicago in the fall of 1991, starting my career as an auditor at Ernst & Young. I wore cheap suits, observed what it took to work in a white-collar environment, and quickly learned the fundamentals of business. But I hated the job from the day I started. I knew that I didn't want to spend the work third of my life this way, and that I wouldn't stay there very long.

After two years, I leveraged my CPA to get a better job as a junior analyst at a Wall Street investment bank called Lehman Brothers. I read *Liar's Poker* and watched *Pretty Woman* before my first interview in a desperate attempt to understand what an investment banker did (the book and the film are both way, way off). I put in hundred-hour work weeks helping companies get bought and sold. I was suddenly making the kind of money that would make my family say, "Must be nice."

I hated that job as well. It was two years of hell and spreadsheets, but it gave me an inside view of the world of finance and company building. Using what I'd learned, I pitched myself as an ideal candidate for the master's program at the Kellogg School of Management at Northwestern University. I headed off to get my MBA convinced I would learn all the secrets of business that had escaped me in the early days of my career.

In business school I wrote down my long-term goal—to own and operate my own business. To be an entrepreneur. But there were two problems. One, I couldn't come up with any good businesses to start. Two, I had a ton of student loan debt that I needed to pay off. So, I bit the bullet and went back to investment banking. My soul ached, but there was one bright spot—rather than go back to New York or Chicago, I decided to head to California.

My real dream would be deferred for a little while, but at least I would be in Silicon Valley, the epicenter of entrepreneurial activity. Every aspect of my conservative Midwestern upbringing was thrown out the window the moment I landed in northern California. I quickly learned how the "valley" worked and immersed myself in every part of it. I loved it.

Within a few years, I found myself living a life that my family back in Ohio could barely imagine. It was the "dot-com" boom, and I was good at investment banking. The job paid me a shocking amount of money, and my professional counterparts were educated and ambitious. Most seemed content with their lives. I felt like I should be content, too. I was only thirty years old, and I had a job and an income right out of the banking scenes from *Wall Street*.

But my job left my soul feeling empty. I realized that money was not going to be the answer to satisfaction in the "work third" of my life.

This desire was tested at the end of 1999. I was working for Morgan Stanley and my annual bonus was $500,000—more money than I could imagine. The firm offered me compensation of $1 million if I stayed on for another year. One year of work! The offer was like the lyrics to Hotel California—accepting it meant that "I could check out anytime I wanted but I could never leave." I had to make a change. I still didn't have any great startup ideas so I decided to do the next best thing—find one to work for instead.

Through a stroke of luck—another consistent theme in my life—I was introduced to legendary entrepreneur Marc Andreessen in 1999. I joined his new managed services provider startup, LoudCloud, as one of the first employees. For two years, I worked with Marc and another amazing leader, Ben Horowitz. I learned in real time what it took to bring a company from an idea all the way through to an Initial Public Offering (IPO).

My job at LoudCloud was more satisfying than the jobs I'd had before because I was finally off the side lines and in "the game." But I wasn't running the show and I wanted to build something on my own. I wanted to lead. I wanted to create culture. I didn't just want to be part of a startup; I wanted to run one. So, at thirty-two, I quit again.

I still didn't have a specific business idea to start but, after some research, determined my best path to entrepreneurship was to buy a small company and grow it. I spent the next two years scouring the United States for a business to acquire, cold calling and sending letters to business owners, and attending every relevant conference I could find.

Luck prevailed again, and I found an incredible company to buy in downtown San Francisco, mere miles from where I was living at the time. With money from a group of investors, I purchased ServiceSource in 2003 and finally began my entrepreneurial journey. Finally, I was chasing my dream.

Okay, pause.

I bet at this point you're a little confused. *Didn't he just say in the introduction that this book isn't a memoir?*

Well, first of all, it's my book, and I already noted my lack of attention to detail.

Seriously, though, it's important for you to understand my journey, because at this point I'd started to realize that I wasn't alone. An old friend of mine was also starting to really chase his own dream—not to become an entrepreneur, or to find fulfillment and satisfaction in life.

No, his dream was to completely mess with my mind and try to derail my efforts every step of the way.

His name? Mr. Monkey.

# ☞ CHAPTER TWO ☜

# MY LIFELONG FRENEMY, MR. MONKEY

*"'Now run along and play, but don't get into trouble.' George promised to be good. But it is easy for little monkeys to forget."*

—H.A REY, *CURIOUS GEORGE*

In the spring of 2003, sixteen years after I first heard that mattress commercial, I was a first-time CEO getting ready for my inaugural company all-hands presentation to our small but growing employee base. I had been waiting all my life for this moment. I barely slept the night before, tossing and turning in anticipation.

We rented a restaurant for the event a few blocks from our office. I walked to it by myself in order to mentally review the main parts of my speech. I didn't want to go with the buzzword-bingo talking points or a boring description of the strategy and growth plans for the business. Rather, I wanted to speak passionately about the vision I had for the company's culture. I hoped to inspire the small team that was working tirelessly for me.

As I got closer to the restaurant, a large hairy beast suddenly came sprinting across the street, waving his arms at me, his hands full of index cards. It was all in my head, of course, but for a moment, it seemed as real as the sun. The image made me stop in my tracks. The large monkey swung his arms around in circles, jumped up and down, and yelled at me aggressively.

*"Do you really want to be vulnerable? This is your first speech to the employees. Are you nuts? Act the part. Don't show any weakness. Play it down the middle for goodness' sake. You're the damn CEO—don't be an idiot!"*

The vision ended before I could utter a word in response. Instantly, my confidence was shaken. Was he right? Should I go with a more scripted and corporate version of my speech? It was so tempting to play it safe. Truth be told, I was learning on the job, and I really *didn't* know what I was doing leading the company.

Walking to the small makeshift stage, my hands trembling, I turned to face the eager crowd. Summoning all my courage, I chose to ignore Mr. Monkey and began speaking from my heart.

"When I was seventeen years old, I heard a radio commercial from a mattress company, and it changed my life," I began.

"Hopefully, you're going to spend a third of your life with friends and family, but unless you're independently wealthy, you're going to have to work. The reason I took all this risk and the reason I'm standing here today is that I want that work third to mean something. Not just for me but for everyone at this company. I want all of us to be part of something different and something memorable. I want to build a company that is a great place to work, where we all work as a team and try to do something great. I want this part of our lives to mean something."

I ended by asking all of them—my teammates—to go with me on the journey of making the work third of our lives something special. The speech felt real. It was the most exhilarating moment of my career. I ended the speech with a lame joke about the benefits of "buying a good mattress," but even that couldn't take away the energy in the room. I climbed down from the stage to loud applause from the fifty or so employees in the room. My message had struck a chord. My entrepreneurial journey had officially begun. Goosebumps covered my arms.

## WILL THE REAL MR. MONKEY PLEASE STAND UP?

It's taken a long time (and a lot of therapy), but, over the years, I've built an understanding of my inner voice of self-doubt, and eventually started to personify that voice as a giant, hyperactive monkey who was bound and determined to mess with me.

Before we get much further, I want to make an essential author's note about this primate. It is, in reality, gender-neutral. I call him "Mr." because, in my scrambled brain, he usually shows up as a male monkey. Your monkey, it turns out, is *your* monkey—and therefore can be as diverse as you want him/her/it to be.

Mr. Monkey shit on my plans, poked holes in my dreams, and tried to derail me with every step forward I took. In reality, this hairy, talkative son of a bitch was (and is) my inner voice and critic. For me, the monkey shows up as fear, uncertainty, and doubt. Mr. Monkey likes nothing better than to show up in the worst of times and try desperately to knock me off my path. Or, as in the story above, he encourages me to play it safe rather than take a risk.

Your monkey may manifest as something else. Instead of riding shotgun in your car and poking at all your weak spots, your monkey may show up through sneaky behaviors like procrastination, risk aversion, or a total shutdown of your imagination.

I believe we all have a monkey of self-doubt following us

around. He's a normal part of our human experience. The shit from your past that bounces around in your brain at the worst possible moment is the monkey. Your inner dialogue of self-doubt and insecurity is the monkey. The monkey is incredibly powerful specifically *because* he knows you so well. He knows exactly where to poke to hit your most bruised, sensitive spots with absolute efficiency.

At this point, I'm sure you're thinking, *Is this a business book, or a damn self-help book?* Well, understanding the mental aspect of entrepreneurship requires a mix of both.

Your most vulnerable moments are when the monkey is the most powerful. I almost didn't make it to that stage giving the all-hands presentation because, early on, I started to listen to him too much. In fact, back in 2001, my dream came close to ending before it had even begun—all thanks to the "advice" I was getting from Mr. Monkey.

## ME, MR. MONKEY, AND A SOAP SALESMAN WALK INTO A TEMPORARY OFFICE SPACE

I quit my job at Loudcloud in June of 2001 hell-bent on finally pursuing my entrepreneurial dream. I'd begun to work with a business partner, David Kennedy, whom I met through a mutual friend. David is smart as a whip and suffers no fools, yet has the ability to be charming as hell. It's a powerful combination. As that summer drew to a close, we began raising money from investors with the goal of finding a business to buy and operate.

Everything seemed to be going great. Then 9/11 happened and the whole world was turned on its ear. There's an old saying that fits especially well with entrepreneurship—*if you want to see God's sense of humor, tell her your plans*....

Luckily, we were able to claw together the small amount of money we needed to get us going, and we were off to the races. I was so excited to get started. I'd dreamed of running and growing a business, to drive instead of being just a passenger. All that stood between me and this vision was finding a good business to acquire. A typical day revolved around sorting through a list of 500 or more potential companies to call, hoping to find a welcoming voice on the other end of the line saying, "Well, hello, I was hoping someone like you would call. Why, yes, I would love to sell you my business for a reasonable price!"

Each day, I would drive into the small shared office space we had rented filled with hope and optimism. "This is the day," I'd whisper to myself as I picked up the phone and began my calls.

My initial hopes and reality quickly diverged sharply.

"Hi, my name is Mike, and I'm interested in buying your business." Hang up. Rinse. Repeat.

The magnitude of the risk I had taken—and largely ignored—began to sink in pretty quickly. The process of trying to find a business to buy absolutely sucked. On a good day, I would get hung up on. On a bad day, I would get laughed at or told to go to hell.

2001 slid into 2002, and there seemed to be no end to the bad news in the world. My enthusiasm shifted to trepidation. My trepidation then shifted into *what the hell have I done?*

Three years ago, I had been offered $1 million for a year of work. Two years ago, I was sitting on Marc Andreessen's private jet as he told me about the early days of Netscape and the internet.

Now I was making almost no money, going through a divorce, and desperately trying to stay sane. It felt like all the work and sacrifice I had done to get out of Toledo was lost. Lost because of some stupid dream of running my own business. As icing on the cake, my mom—the person who mattered the most in my life—had been diagnosed with cancer, and none of the treatments she was undertaking seemed to be working.

*What the hell have I done?* I thought as I hung up the phone after another dead-end conversation. I needed some coffee.

The only problem with getting coffee at the tiny shared office was that I had to walk past a traveling soap salesman who sat at a rental desk a few yards away from mine hawking industrial cleaners over the phone. John's cubicle was next to the coffee station, and if he caught you and struck up a conversation, you were done for. He was a *talker*. Middle-aged and balding, he looked and acted the part of corporate stiff. I tried to time my coffee run as he started one of his sales calls—I wanted nothing to do with his typical "man talk" about sports, women, and weekend plans. But my timing was no match for his innate ability to sniff out a mark.

As I was pouring cheap powdered creamer into my watery coffee, I'd heard John's salesman voice, "How's things, Mike?"

"How's things? How *are* things, John? You really want to know *how are things?*"

Without warning, Mr. Monkey appeared, jumping up and down, getting right in John's face, screeching.

*"How's things? He grew up dirt poor in Ohio. Got himself edu-cated. Got a great job. Then another one. And another one. At one point, he had a chance to make $1 million a year, John. All that work to climb out of Toledo, and he threw it away to sit here in this office, smelling your leaky bottles of bathroom cleaner and getting hung up on fifty times a day. He barely knows his business partner. His mom has cancer. His mar-riage is over. This morning, he ran eight miles to try to sweat*

*out a hangover, then he talked to his ex-wife about arbitra-
tion and had a call with his mother about whether she should
continue chemotherapy. This single cup of shitty coffee he's
allotted is one of the bright spots in his day. How the hell do
you think things are, John?"*

But, of course, John couldn't see Mr. Monkey. He was only
there for me, cutting right to the core of all my insecuri-
ties. That's the thing about Mr. Monkey; he doesn't deal in
generalities. He knows you too well. Understands all your
weaknesses. That's why it hurts so much. That's why we fight
so hard to try and push him away.

"Hey, John," I said. "Yeah, good weekend. BBQ. Football. Go
Niners."

Then I walked back to my desk, attempted to shove Mr. Monkey's observations back deep down in my gut, picked up my
phone, and started dialing for dollars again.

## HEY, MR. MONKEY...WE NEED TO TALK

On one particularly awful day at my temporary desk near the
soap salesman, after a phone list full of *nos* and hang-ups, I
got in the car feeling exhausted and defeated. The lack of
progress we were making on finding a business to buy and
the weight of my career decisions started to hit me like a
ton of bricks.

When I started my entrepreneurial journey, I knew I was taking a risk. But after a year of trying to buy a business—with no good prospects in sight—the weight of my decision began to sink in. The magnitude of the risk I had taken on was much greater than I had expected. With this as a backdrop, Mr. Monkey was having a field day. No longer a quiet voice, he had turned into a screaming maniac, filling my head.

In the spring of 2002, our conversation came to a head...in my head.

As I looked in the mirror after a long day of rejections and hang-ups, I finally asked myself the critical questions: *What was I doing? And was all of this worth it? Should I give up on this silly dream?*

As usual, Mr. Monkey chimed right in with his point of view, starting in on me, shouting, *"What the hell are you doing? You had a real job! Why did you leave? You could have been making millions, but you chose this? Time to give this silly dream up. Maybe you can get your old banking job back."*

This time, instead of trying to tune him out, I looked him square in the eyes and said, "Fine. Let me have it."

*"This is too hard for you,"* Mr. Monkey said. *"Look at you! You're exhausted. You're not taking care of yourself. I don't think you can handle this entrepreneur stuff."*

"This is hard because I haven't done it before," I said. "Investment banking was hard when I first started, too, but then I figured it out."

*"What if you can't find a business to buy? Everyone keeps hanging up on you! What if you fail?"*

"I only need one *yes*," I said. "I have a lot to offer a business."

*"OK, but what about this partner of yours?"* Uh-oh, the bastard was starting to get personal now. *"You two are very different. I bet you screw this up. Based on your personal life—for example—it is pretty clear that partnerships aren't your strength. Even if you do find a business, I bet you and David will never be able to work together."*

"Well, yes, he *is* quite different from me," I acknowledged. "But that just means we'll complement each other, instead of overlapping in skills."

*"What about... what about..."* Mr. Monkey stammered. He was starting to look kind of sleepy.

"Hey," I said, "you're just self-doubt. I hear what you're saying, but I'm going to keep doing this."

*"Whatever,"* Mr. Monkey said, stifling a yawn. *"Suit yourself."*

He ambled out of the room, curled up on the couch, and fell into a peaceful slumber. Finally, it seemed, he was giving me a break. Maybe this was the only way to shut him up, if just for a minute. *Talk to him. Hear what he has to say. Then keep moving forward.*

## SPOILER ALERT: MR. MONKEY ISN'T GOING ANYWHERE

Through my time as an entrepreneur, my work now with Next Coast Ventures, and discussions with incredibly successful entrepreneurs, I've learned that there is one unfortunate truth about the monkey. It doesn't matter if you've successfully run a multi-billion-dollar business or you're just thinking of turning your passion into a career, everyone has a monkey. I've outlined some universal truths about the monkey in the Monkey Minders at the end of this chapter; make sure you take these truths seriously, because they're not going away.

Your monkey probably doesn't sound exactly like my Uncle Joe, but maybe he sounds like your seventh-grade teacher, or your mother, or your first boss. Everyone has their particular brand of self-doubt, but everyone has moments of feeling like they don't know what the hell they're doing.

What your voice sounds like and what the voice says really doesn't matter. How you manage your monkey will make all the difference in your journey. The difference between success and failure. The difference between Starbucks and Joe's Coffee Shop. Between McDonald's and Sam's Burger Shop. Nike and…okay, you get it. The point is that we all have these voices and they are individual to each of us. The only difference is how we react to the voices.

The motivation to raise your hand and become an entrepreneur comes from a small voice inside you that says, "I can do it." Something will go wrong, usually pretty quickly, and Mr. Monkey will turn to you and say, *"No you can't."* The real challenge is to reframe that voice into something you can use. To make you stronger, more focused, and aware.

The goal is to start to see Mr. Monkey like a great opponent in your entrepreneurial chess game. When he makes a good move (or highlights a particular weakness) you could ignore him or wish he would go away. Neither will work. The goal is to say, "Well played," examine the chess board, and plot a new route to victory.

When you listen to what the monkey has to say instead of trying to drown out his voice, you can use your logic and reason to work through the doubt he's peddling. The SHAPE formula is focused on dealing with Mr. Monkey and providing you with specific and actionable ways to deal with the hairy beast. He or she isn't going anywhere—but that doesn't mean they'll win the day. It's your time to shine. So let's get after the bastard, starting with the first letter in the SHAPE formula: getting some **S**elf-awareness.

## MONKEY MINDERS: TRUTHS
## ABOUT THE MONKEY

- *The monkey is real.* Well, maybe *real* isn't quite accurate, but what he/she/it symbolizes is certainly very real. The monkey represents the mental obstacles that stand between you and your dreams.

- *Everybody has a monkey.* The subject matter and tone may be different, but everyone struggles with this internal voice. You are not alone—every great entrepreneur has a voice that told them to quit, to give up, or to not even begin in the first place. Every single one.

- *It's important to recognize what the monkey is and what it isn't.* For me, the monkey typically shows up as fear, uncertainty, and doubt. What the monkey represents might be different for you. The key is to recognize the monkey as a mindset or emotion you have control over—*not* the other way around. While very powerful and not to be overlooked, the monkey is only as strong as you allow it to be.

- *The secret is to invite Mr. Monkey in for a chat.* You can learn a great deal from Mr. Monkey if you have the right mindset. Openness about the monkey is the only way to see the obstacles it represents for what they really are and what they *aren't.* Once you do that, you can begin to develop the mental toughness that is crucial for success.

- *The monkey never goes away.* How the monkey shows up for you will change as time goes on, but trying to get him to go away completely is a fool's errand. How you manage the monkey is the key to your success. The SHAPE formula is specifically designed to help you get the mental edge necessary to manage the beast.

# ☞ CHAPTER THREE ☜

# S-SELF (AS IN KNOW THYSELF)

*Yesterday I was clever, so I wanted to change the world. Today I am wise, so I am changing myself.*

—JALAL AD-DIN MUHAMMAD RUMI

Imagine your friend Bob comes to you and says, "I want to run a marathon." He knows you ran a marathon years ago and he wants your advice on how to get started training. Bob has never run before, and he's not in great shape, but running a marathon has always been on his bucket list, and he's decided it's finally time.

How would you best help him? You wouldn't just show him a video of Eliud Kipchoge of Kenya finishing the Berlin marathon in two hours, then send him to the athletic store to buy sneakers, shouting, "Good luck, Bob! It's going to be so much fun. You'll be great!" That would be absurd and irresponsible, right? At best, Bob's going to give up; at worst, he's going to hurt himself.

This is *exactly* the level of guidance that most entrepreneurs typically receive about mental strength as they start their journey.

What your aspiring runner friend Bob needs to get started on his marathon is for a good, helpful friend to say, "Here's a sixteen-week course for beginners. It will sound basic, but this plan will tell you when to run, how far to run, and how to rest and recover." A productive, comprehensive marathon plan will also instruct Bob on how to get enough sleep, optimize his diet, hydrate properly, and mentally prepare to run for four to six hours without stopping. Inspiration is useful, but inspiration is not a plan for the path forward, and inspiration won't get Bob—or you—to the finish line.

In your entrepreneur journey, I'm going to be your good, helpful friend. I designed the SHAPE Method to be your no-bullshit training program for the mental aspect of being an entrepreneur. You can do this, but it's going to be hard. It's going to suck sometimes—the same way it will suck for Bob when he has to drag his ass out of bed at 6 a.m. to go for a training run. But the hard work will be worth it, and I believe in you.

## NOT JUST A BEER MAN—THE BEST BEER MAN

"Beer here! Who needs a cold beer? Beer here!" I yelled to the crowd as I scaled the steep steps of the upper deck of Riverfront Stadium on a surprisingly warm early winter Sunday afternoon. It was the Cincinnati Bengals' very last Sunday of the regular season. It was my senior year in college, so hopefully it was also my last Sunday selling beer.

The job had served me well. I had taken the part-time job three years ago simply because I needed the money to help pay for college. So every Sunday I would make the one-hour drive to Cincinnati, pop in one of my self-help cassettes and imagine my life ahead. For the past four years, I had become addicted to these audio tapes and listened to them nonstop. When I walked across campus with headphones on, friends assumed I was listening to the latest from The Smiths or N.W.A. Little did they know that I was ingesting self-help wisdom from the likes of Denis Waitley and Earl Nightingale.

These tapes had been instrumental in what was called "mental reprogramming"—essentially changing the self-talk (or monkey talk) in my head. In layman's terms, these tapes slowly replaced my Uncle Joe and Grandma's voices with a talk track that said, "You can do it" and "Think positive."

As I approached the football stadium, I'd put on my blue polyester uniform, set a goal for the day, and mentally transformed myself into someone else—the *best beer man ever.* This approach allowed me to learn a ton about sales and human nature, and it helped me pay my way through college. But now it was time to move on. I couldn't wait to graduate and get on with my new life. However, on this particular Sunday, I was still a beer salesman.

"BEER HERE! Get your ICE COLD BEER HERE! Who wants one?" I shouted.

Someone called out, "Hey, Beer Man, bring me one, would you?"

I followed the direction of the voice, and made my way up the stairs, too busy watching my feet to look at the person shouting. I was carrying two cases of beer to maximize my sales potential, so I had to be careful with my footing.

"Hey, Beer Man!" the voice called again. It sounded familiar. "Shit, Smerklo, is that you? What the heck are you doing selling beer?"

It was Jeff Kubaki, a guy I'd played basketball with back in high school. We'd gone to the same college, too, but too much weed and beer had gotten the better of him, and he dropped out after our sophomore year and moved back to Toledo. What the hell was he doing here?

"Hey Jeff," I said, trying to act like I wasn't embarrassed to be seen in my uniform. "What's up, man? What kind of beer can I get you?"

"Well, shit, I'll take a Budweiser. Dude, what are you doing? Still in school? Looks like it's working out *great* for you!"

The mocking tone in his voice was one I had heard over and over the past four years from friends and coworkers every time I went back to Toledo. Nicknames like "college boy" highlighted ways I was changing in the eyes of people who had never considered leaving the neighborhood. Aunts and uncles shared pearls of wisdom such as, "Don't ever forget your roots, boy," as they became increasingly jealous of my changing station in life. I knew I didn't completely fit in with my college peers, and this constant commentary from people in Toledo made me feel as if the life I'd come from was rejecting me as well. I didn't know if I would ever find a place of belonging.

A more mature version of myself would be able to recognize Jeff's petty jealousy and understand he was likely dealing with his own inner Mr. Monkey. But for now, it felt like Jeff was carrying a flag for all the other people who had poked fun at me for trying to better myself.

Anyone who has left an old environment in order to get to a better station in life knows this feeling. It stings like hell.

I grabbed one of the longneck bottles of Budweiser from

the top case I was carrying and poured the beer into the plastic cup. I had learned to hold the cup at a forty-five-degree angle to deliver the beer free of foam in the quickest way possible. Typically, I would hold out the prized beer, offer a big smile and say, "Cold beer HERE," changing the emphasis to the last word in order to increase the likeliness of a tip. Not this time. I handed Jeff his beer and quickly glanced past him.

"Seriously, dude, you should move back to Toledo," Jeff said as he took a long sip of the freshly poured Budweiser. "I just got a job at the Jeep plant. Twenty bucks an hour, and I barely do shit. Better than selling beer for sure. I can put in a good word with the foreman if you want."

"Thanks, Jeff," I said. "I appreciate it, but I'm all set. I'd love to catch up with you, but I'd better get back to it."

"You, too, man. You, too. Man, I can't wait to tell the guys at home that college boy is selling beers at the Bengals game!"

Jeff paid for his beer but skipped the tip.

"Good to see you, man," I said, relieved to walk away. I tried to put the conversation out of my mind, but I was so mad I could barely stand it. The anger quickly morphed into massive embarrassment and self-doubt. I worked for a few hours more before turning in my uniform and walking to my car for the long drive back to campus. I had expected to be thrilled to end this chapter in my life, looking forward to what the future held for me in Chicago after graduation. But now I was paralyzed by rage.

As I started the drive home, I could feel Denis Waitley's face on the cover of the *Seeds of Greatness* audiobook case mocking me. I couldn't bring myself to listen. I suddenly doubted all of that self-help bullshit—had I only believed my ability to get out of Toledo because of a bunch of tapes full of self-indulgent mumbo jumbo? Could I make it work in Chicago? *Should* I be trying to get a job at the Jeep plant instead? My inner voice was going crazy.

And suddenly, there was Mr. Monkey in the passenger seat again. He bounced up and down with his excitement to sling self-doubt and ridicule all over my car.

*"Why do you think you can get out? Jeff couldn't. And look at him. He's fine. Twenty dollars an hour at the Jeep plant? You could do a lot with that kind of money in Toledo."*

"I know, but I want something different for my life," I said.

Mr. Monkey grinned. *"And people in hell want ice water."*

By the time I got close to campus, I was flushed with anxiety and self-doubt, uncomfortable in my skin. I couldn't fathom going back to campus and walking into my fraternity as if everything was fine. Over the past four years, I had tried so hard to hide my roots. As part of my transformation from poor kid to articulate, educated, fraternity guy, I'd spent hard-earned money on preppy clothes and a fashionable haircut, and worked to be less crass with my choice of words. I'd even removed the two ear piercings that I'd gotten in high school. But I was an imposter, and I knew it. Desperately seeking some way to clear my head, I pulled over to the side of the road a few miles from campus.

While I'd listened to Denis Waitley's tapes over and over for years, I'd always resisted doing any of the written exercises he prescribed. Maybe that was the problem, I thought, grasping for hope. Maybe if I did the exercises, I'd be able to shut that damn monkey up. I found an old notebook in my backseat and grabbed a pen, starting what felt like a list Denis Waitley would prescribe.

At the top of the pages, I wrote *What I Know about Myself*, followed by a bulleted list:

- I am competitive and hate to lose.
- I have a massive need to prove myself to others.
- I am a pretty smart guy. Not the smartest, but a good combination of street and book smart.
- I am extremely motivated by money.
- People like me, but I have a hard time trusting others.

- I like to be in charge. I hate being told what to do by anyone. Anyone...
- I like public communication and particularly selling.
- I get embarrassed easily and care tremendously what others think about me.
- I refuse to cheat and won't play outside of the rules of a game.
- I care more about my own success than just about anything else.
- I love team wins, but my personal success is more important than team success.

When I read this list today, I am filled with amusement and a touch of embarrassment. Funny at how accurate this list was thirty years ago—and a bit shocking how little it has changed. This list provided the twenty-two-year-old version of me a foundation for becoming an entrepreneur.

This was my first real attempt at self-awareness and it was incredibly important for me in three distinct ways. First, it showed me how hard it is to break out of an old way of thinking. Second, it made it clear to me that I was different, and my perspective on risk, opportunity, and the impact I wanted to have in life was unique in comparison to my friends and peers. Third, it quieted Mr. Monkey, for at least a few moments.

I bet you can relate. Maybe you've always felt different than others around you, even if just a little. Maybe you have struggled to break out of an old way of thinking. Perhaps Mr. Monkey is even in your head at *this very moment* telling you not to take risks. If that's the case, it's important to remember that, as an entrepreneur, you *are* different, and that's a good thing. It's critical to develop the self-awareness of what drives you, and understand why even when you landed your "dream job" you still always seem to want more...

## YOU MIGHT BE AN ENTREPRENEUR IF...

Imagine: You've landed your dream job at a design firm, and for the first few months, it was everything you'd hoped it would be. But as time went on, your enthusiasm started to... not so much *wane* but be dulled by what feels like constant inaction. As soon as you got up to speed on the status quo, you started seeing where that status quo isn't quite everything it was cracked up to be.

It's the last Friday of June. Dan, the owner of Dan Jones Design, is running the quarterly meeting. This quarter, the main topic on the agenda is growth strategies.

You find yourself thinking about what you would do differently if you were in charge. In fact, you're *always* thinking about what you would do differently if you were in charge. There's a running list in your head of all the improvements you could make that you started a year and a half ago. You're still relatively new to the company, so you're reticent about sharing these ideas. Some of your team members have been with Dan's company for over twenty years. Everyone else seems excited about these marginal improvements, and you don't want to rock the boat, but you can't help but feel frustrated. Dan Jones Design does excellent work, but the company could have a much broader reach if everyone thought bigger.

You have some ideas you'd like to talk with Dan about. You've been looking into the potential for expansion and the customer base you could reach with more resources. You take a moment to plan your approach and work up your nerve, but before you have a chance to share your ideas, Dan glances at his watch. You check your phone. It's 4:59.

"Well, I want to respect your time. We've had a great session today," Dan says, calling the meeting to a close.

Millie, the office manager, stops by your desk while you're packing up to go home. "Hi, sweetheart," Millie says, flashing you a warm smile. "It was Gloria's birthday, and there's still a little cake left in the break room. You should go get a piece."

"Thanks," you say. "Hey, Millie, I'm curious. Was that meeting satisfying and meaningful to you?"

Millie looks at you like you might have grown an extra head.

"Sure, I guess. It's always fun for us to get some good face-to-face time together."

"You've been here from the start, and I was wondering...." You stammer a bit as you get ready to ask the real question on your mind. "Do you—do you think Dan would ever consider growing the company faster? Maybe entering a new market?"

"Dan *has* grown the company! There were only four of us when we started out on that old dining room table in the apartment over his garage twenty-five years ago," her eyes a little misty. "The economy isn't great out there, but Dan did good. Look at all of us now! Oh, I'm thankful to have such a nice place to work."

You slump in your office chair. The opportunities for growth and improvement are obvious, but no one seems interested in pushing just a little bit harder. You know that after this meeting there might be a few small things that will change, but the company isn't going to implement innovative growth strategies on a large scale. Competition may be coming, but Dan Jones Design won't be prepared. No one else seems concerned, and it makes you feel truly alone.

Everyone is packing up to go home, but you stay at your desk and write an email to Dan. *Great job with the meeting today. I know we ran out of time, but I have several ideas on how we could grow the business, and I'd love the chance to discuss them with you and the team.* You're inspired. It's a goosebumps kind of moment. You think back to that movie with Tom Cruise as a sports agent and that manifesto he wrote one night to his entire company. What was that movie called? Something about showing the money. Maybe that can be the subject line on your email? *Brilliant,* you think, as your fingers fly across the keyboard.

Your heart starts racing. You lay out the plans you came up with for increasing client outreach and expanding the team. You write and rewrite, wanting to set the perfect tone to get Dan excited.

By the time you look up from your computer, everyone else is gone, and Russell, the night janitor, is walking around emptying garbage cans. You're about to hit send but decide you'll save your email in the drafts folder and send it on Monday, so you can add any ideas you might have over the weekend. You finally call it a night, pack up your things, wave goodnight to Russell, and walk out to your car.

On the drive home, your car is full of monkeys.

A monkey wearing a Dan Jones Design golf shirt scolds you. *"Don't mess it up, man! We've got it good! And Dan's been running this company for a long time, and he's certainly done a pretty good job. Why do you doubt someone who runs a very successful firm? Who do you think you are?"*

"*Hey, the economy's pretty tight,*" the next monkey says, her charm bracelet jangling as she pats your shoulder. "*Why don't you just shut up and be happy you have a good job!*"

"*Be glad you don't have to worry about any of that,*" the third monkey says, looking at his watch. "*It's not your responsibility.*"

"I guess it is up to Dan to figure this stuff out," you say, sighing.

The three monkeys love seeing your stance weaken. They pile on, shrieking all at once.

"*Why would you want all the responsibility of running a company?*"

"*Why are you always so unsatisfied? Can't you just be happy with the way things are?*"

"*I heard 90 percent of all startups fail. Why do you think you are better than Dan Jones?!*"

"*And remember what happened to Tom Cruise in that movie? The name of it was Jerry Fucking Maguire, dipshit. NOT Show Me the Money! And Tom Cruise got fired after he sent out that manifesto!*"

"Yeah, I guess you're right," you say to them. "What the hell do I know? Dan's been running this business for twenty-five years."

Then another voice enters your head, so solidly your own. *Shit, why can't I be satisfied? Why do I keep dreaming about doing my own thing? What is wrong with me?*

The monkeys chatter happily, certain that they've won. But even as you agree with them, something in your gut is telling you that those monkeys are wrong.

Remember the Jeff Foxworthy bit where he told the audience they might be a redneck if they followed specific patterns of behavior? Well, if this story rang true for you, you might be an entrepreneur. There are probably a hundred different ways of being an entrepreneur, but the primary connection is that you feel different, and you feel motivated by that difference.

The driving force behind that feeling of difference may vary from one entrepreneur to the next, but the thing we all share is that we're motivated to have an impact. To build something. To make a difference. The first step on the journey of entrepreneurship is to get to know yourself a bit more, to recognize that you are different, and to realize that this is a good thing. The world needs you now more than ever.

## FIRST THINGS FIRST: WRITE YOUR LIST

Remember, we all have a monkey—every single one of us. Self-awareness isn't easy for anyone, and when you're first coming up, the monkey is going to try to drag you down by focusing on the extremes of your strengths and weaknesses. The monkey is going to tell you you're either really smart, or really stupid; the most talented person you know, or the biggest loser. As you well know, you're neither—you land somewhere in the middle. All of us do. Everyone is very good at some things and not so good at some other things.

*"You suck at organization,"* Mr. Monkey might observe as you write your business plan.

"Yes, organizational skills aren't my strong point, but I'm not afraid of chaos, which makes me well-suited to projects requiring constellation thinking. And thanks for reminding me—I need to update the Team section in my business plan to include hiring an executive who is a process junkie."

Writing down a list of what you know about yourself, like I did, is the first step toward self-awareness. While it may feel scary to take such a direct look at yourself, acknowledging your strengths and weaknesses will ultimately help you interact with the monkey in a productive way. Self-awareness enhances your immunity to both sycophantic advice and unhelpful criticism. So make your list—but there's one important rule. You must be *brutally* honest when you make it.

Don't worry, no one else is going to see the list. It's just for you. Once you write down this "self-inventory," take a look and consider how the attributes listed filter into your behavior. Once you fully understand your strengths and weaknesses, you can figure out how to use them to your advantage. You'll also quickly see what gaps you have—which is normal, we all have gaps—and build a strategy to bridge them as quickly as possible. If you're going to be an entrepreneur, your full self will be on display more than you can ever imagine. So you might as well get to know yourself now before everyone else does, right?

In working with entrepreneurs at the companies we've invested in through Next Coast Ventures, we've seen a wide range of traits that make a great entrepreneur. In fact, one of my biggest surprises in moving into venture capital was that there aren't many magic-bullet traits shared by successful entrepreneurs—for the most part, their characteristics are without commonality.

But there is one common trait that we've seen universally across a very diverse group, and that's self-awareness. It seems to be the single determining factor between success and failure. It's *that* important.

## MONKEY MINDERS #1: HOW TO BUILD SELF-AWARENESS

- *Start with a list.* I still use the B.A.G. methodology I learned so long ago from Denis Waitley's *Seeds of Greatness* audio tapes. It sounds corny as heck, but every year I write down my blessings, accomplishments, and goals. The *Blessings* section reminds me of all my good fortunes. *Accomplishments* is a tally of what I have been able to do with these gifts. My *Goals* list changes every year, and always provides me energy and focus.

- *Make another list.* This time write down what you like to do and what you are good at. Then write down the opposites. Get curious about what the list is telling you about yourself. This two-by-two grid is one of the most useful tools I have ever experienced. By listing what I am good at and what I am not good at, I get clarity on my skillsets. By listing what I like to do and what I don't like to do, I get a sense of where to put my energy—and when I'll need to seek help or find additional resources.

- *Test your self-reporting.* We all have shortcomings and blind spots. Don't take Mr. Monkey's input as fact. Find a trusted professional peer (or peers) and ask them two simple questions: *What do you think are the two to three things that I am really good at professionally? What do you think I am not so good at in the work environment?* Make sure you choose peers who can give you objective feedback. Promise to refrain from getting angry or offended, and keep that promise. When you seek external input and assessment, you may be shocked by the areas where your self-awareness is dead on and where your blind spots are most prominent.

- *Consider your resources.* After you've worked on self-assessment and sought feedback from trusted peers, start thinking about the people you know who may be able to help you build upon your strengths and those who may be able to help you mitigate your shortcomings. For example, if you're great at writing but unsure of how to tailor your skills for marketing, reaching out to a specialist could help you hone your skills. Or if you've discovered budgeting to be a constant source of frustration, you may want to reach out to an accountant for help. This is the real blessing of self-awareness. It provides you with a foundation to build upon and a path forward to get some help (which is the topic of the next chapter).

# CHAPTER FOUR

# H–HELP

*"Keep away from people who try to belittle your ambitions. Small people always do that, but the really great make you feel that you, too, can become great."*

—MARK TWAIN

Getting help is one of the least talked about aspects of entrepreneurship but fortunately, one of the easiest to put into practice.

For me, the hardest part was actually asking, because I always thought of needing help as a sign of weakness. Any time I felt unsure about my path forward, I could hear Uncle Joe saying, "Suck it up! Be a man," inside my head, and I would avoid asking for much-needed advice out of the fear of seeming soft.

For many leaders, entrepreneurs, and innovators, asking for

help isn't in our DNA, but failing to pull on outside resources to tackle tough situations can be perilous. Luckily for me, I *mostly* overcame this before it killed my entrepreneurial career, but it was a close call. How close? The next story will give you a sense.

## DON'T HIRE A COKE ADDICT

A year after buying ServiceSource, the business was doing great. Despite our lack of experience and expertise, David and I were growing the company faster than we'd expected. Everyone on the team was working hard, and we had a big market that needed what we were selling. I was personally tasked with signing new customers, which is one of the most important jobs in the early days of an entrepreneurial endeavor. While the results were good, it was becoming clear that our future success would be dependent on our ability to get a trained, professional sales force in place. Our problem was simple: no one on the team, including me, had any idea how to build a sales team.

After discussing the situation carefully with our Board of Directors, we determined that the best strategy would be to hire a veteran executive to serve as head of sales. I faked confidence in the board meeting and expressed my assurance in our ability to attract and recruit a "true professional."

Inside, I wasn't just nervous about our chances of recruiting the right person; I was scared shitless. Up until this point, I had only really hired a few entry-level employees. Now, I had to recruit, hire, and train a "real" executive. *Oh, shit.*

We searched extensively, and I finally came across a fantastic candidate. On paper, it seemed like Jim was perfect for the job. He had the level and depth of experience we were looking for. He was also available, having taken a few years off after his last company sold, so we wouldn't have to poach him from another business.

I flew to San Diego, where Jim was living at the time, to recruit him. I did all the right reference checks, even driving to Los Altos to have lunch with his former CEO. She gave me a glowing reference.

"This guy is going to change the trajectory of our business," I told my board. They approved the hire, and Jim started at the beginning of May.

Right off the bat, we noticed a few odd things about Jim. He would fly home to San Diego for the weekend, usually leaving Thursday night and returning to San Francisco on Monday. He was often late. He always seemed a little bit tired and would joke about his "fun weekend" wearing him out. He chugged excessive amounts of coffee. A few weeks in, he came in with strange cuts on his fingers. He said he'd been doing some house projects, but something about the defensiveness of his tone when he answered felt off. Sometimes, Jim was missing in action for a day or two without an explanation.

The simplest thing to do would have been to have an open and measured discussion with Jim to see what was actually going on. That plan works on the assumption that Mr. Monkey wasn't inside my head, reminding me that I had never done this job before. However, Mr. Monkey was working overtime to remind me that there was only one truly experienced executive in the company (and his name wasn't Mike). I'd also just finished reading a book about the perils of micromanaging. Out of a fear of stepping on Jim's toes, I stepped back completely and let his behavior continue, despite my growing concerns.

In June, I left for my first vacation in years, taking a scuba diving trip in Antigua with my girlfriend, Abby. We'd specifically chosen a quaint little lodge that had no room phone or cell coverage. Only my mother and David (my business partner) had the front desk number in case of emergencies, and we were otherwise blissfully off the grid.

This vacation was a huge deal for me. It was the first time since we'd bought the business that I'd taken off more than a half-day on the weekend. Those first eighteen months were a flat-out grind. It was shocking that I had even been able to sustain a personal relationship, given my daily routine.

Every part of my day focused on growing the business and being successful as a CEO. I was pouring my heart into my work and neglecting almost everything else. I had a two-bedroom apartment in the Marina District in San Francisco, and I'd never even gotten around to furnishing it. I had a bed, and in the living room, I had a TV on a stand and an Aeron chair. No couch. No dining table.

Every weekday was the same. The alarm rang at 5:45 in the morning and I stumbled out of bed, put on my work-out clothes, and headed to the fridge. Reaching around the half-empty Chinese food containers, I'd find my Red Bull (no time for coffee) to help kickstart my day. I'd grab my gym bag, drive to the Bay Club, and work out like a madman. By 7:45 I was in the office at my desk, and I'd work until seven or eight o'clock every night. Then I'd go home and do it again the next day. On Friday and Saturday night, I'd drink until I couldn't stand up. On Monday, I'd start all over again.

Now, with Jim hired and getting ramped up, I was desperately in need of a break.

As Abby and I settled into the lodge, the lapping waves and soft ocean breeze quickly drained the stress away. Our first day was beautiful. I drank actual coffee. We spent time on the beach in the sun, and I felt my life force returning. As Abby and I lounged in our beach chairs, cocktails in hand,

I remember saying, "Oh my God, I'd forgotten what living feels like. I might actually read a book!"

When we headed back inside the lodge to change for dinner, the front desk manager came running up to me with a pink piece of paper. It was a note from David, my trusted business partner: *Try and call if you can. I need to discuss something with you.* David was calm, cool, and collected on the worst of days, so even his understated message told me that something important was up.

It was already seven o'clock in the evening, and we were about to go to dinner. This was before smartphones, and Wi-Fi wasn't available anywhere on the island so I figured I would just call when I could. The next day, we went out for an early morning swim, but we were having such a wonderful time that our morning swim turned into a day at the beach. On our way back to the room, the front desk manager ran toward me again. This time with three pink slips of paper.

Noon—*Mike, please call David.*

Two o'clock—*Mike, David needs to talk to you immediately.*

Four o'clock—*Mike, call me regardless of what time you get this. David.*

I called David immediately.

"Hey," he said, "I'm sorry to bother you, but we had an important sales meeting, and Jim missed it. He was unreachable all day Monday and just blew off the meeting today. No one can find him, and it has been three days since we've heard from him. We finally got a hold of him right before you called, but he was incoherent and unapologetic. We need to fire him."

I trusted David completely and didn't think twice about his rationale. I knew we had to act quickly, and I immediately agreed with his recommendation.

We didn't go home early, but I was drenched in remorse and embarrassment. Even though I was still in Antigua, it didn't feel like a vacation anymore. When I sat on the beach next to Abby, holding the book I'd planned to read, I couldn't even focus on the words. I felt like Mr. Monkey was stretched out on a neighboring lounge chair, laughing at me while he sipped a daiquiri.

*"I knew you couldn't handle this, Mike,"* he said, lowering his sunglasses to give me a hard stare. *"You have been over your skis since day one. What do you know about hiring an executive?"* It was hard to argue with the hairy beast even as he sunned himself in a bathing suit that looked like the hideous gray weenie bikini my Uncle Joe wore on Sunday Fun Day back in Ohio.

I had, as my first real executive hire, chosen a raging coke addict.

The dread seeped in and wouldn't leave me. Even though I'd presented Jim as the second coming in sales, when I got home, I'd have to go back to the board and let them know we fired him. We'd also have to tell all the customers he'd met that he wasn't working for us anymore, and update the employees at the next all-hands. We couldn't even give any details as to why we were making this change.

We emailed a few times with Jim to make sure he was okay, but then we lost contact. I don't know what became of him. I hope he checked into rehab.

It was a horrible experience, but I learned three essential rules that somehow never came up in business school:

1.  Don't hire coke addicts. It turns out that they're not very reliable.
2.  You're going to make mistakes. Lots of them.
3.  Get help.

## COACH BILL

I would love to tell you that after my misstep on Jim's hiring, I figured it all out and hired a fantastic replacement. Truth is, I screwed up the head of sales hire two more times. I kept trying to solve the problem by myself, but I didn't know how to find the right hire, even though I felt like I had to pretend I did. Firing that third head of sales made me worry that I wouldn't live long enough professionally to make it to number four. Finally, I realized I needed to talk to Coach Bill.

Bill Campbell was a Silicon Valley legend who everyone called "Coach." He was a wise and wonderful man. In the book *Trillion Dollar Coach*, Bill is credited with helping to build some of Silicon Valley's greatest companies—including Apple, Google, and Intuit—and creating over a trillion dollars in market value. Bill had been a college football player and coach, but his real calling was advising the best and brightest entrepreneurs in both formal and informal capacities. Bill was a legendary advisor to Steve Jobs, Larry Page, and Eric Schmidt, and coached dozens of CEOs and founders. Coach was an amazingly optimistic, no-bullshit kind of guy. A gruff voice made it sound as if he had just chain-smoked an entire pack of cigarettes. He'd been on the board of LoudCloud, and I was fortunate to get to know him while I worked there.

Coach was an investor in a bar called the Old Pro in Palo Alto, where he often held court. Any time I met him for a beer, there was always someone leaving just as I got there, and someone waiting to take my seat when it was time for me to go, each one of us eager for our thirty minutes with Coach.

"Smerklo, you numbnut! Come get a beer!" he shouted when I walked in the bar.

As I sat down next to him, he said, "You look like dog shit. What's going on?"

I took a sip of my beer and thought of how best to bring Coach up to speed on my challenges. Since Jim's "departure" from the company, things had gone from bad to worse. I wasn't sure where to start. My sip of beer turned into half the bottle consumed in one gulp.

"Well, Coach," I said, my voice low with embarrassment, "I just fired my third VP of Sales in less than eighteen months. I have no idea where I'm going to find the right one."

With each of the hires, I'd been certain the person I'd found was exactly what we needed, so now I wasn't sure how to trust my instincts going forward. I didn't know if there were more red flags I should be looking for. I felt like the cat was out of the bag. The emperor had no clothes. And everyone else was bound to find out soon.

"I don't know what I'm doing," I said, "and maybe—"

"Well, who the hell is helping you?" Coach said. "No one knows what they're doing all the time. You need someone to help you."

"What do you mean, who's helping me?" I asked, gulping the rest of my beer and motioning the bar tender for another one. "I am the CEO. We have a recruiting firm to source candidates, but isn't it my job to find our head of sales?"

"Smerklo, you are as dumb as a post. I mean: who is *your* coach, Mike? Who's your mentor? What are you doing? You know tons of people who have been in your shoes. Are you calling them?"

"Well, no," I stammered. "I don't have time, Bill. I've got to hire a new head of sales. I can barely keep up most days, and with this latest screwup, I feel like there's no way I can possibly catch up. I don't have time for help."

Hearing myself say those words was the beginning of my attitude adjustment. I knew how pathetic and wrong it sounded. I'd seen other people fall into the same trap. The pressing issue seems so overwhelming that you can't conceptualize a way of bridging the gap between your resources and what you need to accomplish. I was too caught up in my own bullshit and couldn't see through the trees.

The beauty of talking to Coach Bill was that he wasn't going to let me get away with that behavior. A buddy would have commiserated. If I'd gone to a different bar with a different friend, I would have drunk my sorrows into submission, only to wake up with a hangover and no solutions the next day.

Coach was all about giving it to me straight. First, he started with one of his catchphrases just to set the stage.

"Smerklo, you are so fucked up you make me look good." He shook his head as he continued. "How the hell are you going to do this without help? There's a bunch of shit you don't know. You're aware that you've never hired a head of sales before this whole scenario. Working harder's not going to get you there. You need someone to tell you what they did and didn't do. And how it worked or didn't work. So, you made a mistake. Everyone makes mistakes. You're not supposed to know everything. That's not your job. Your job is to find mentors. Stop punishing yourself and ask for help."

Hmm, I thought as I left the Old Pro and jumped into my SUV to begin the forty-five-minute crawl back to San Francisco through 101 traffic. Coach's advice was quite different from the words of wisdom I'd been getting from my old buddy Mr. Monkey on the drive down to Palo Alto. Admit when I didn't know something? Seek advice? Show weakness? Those felt like a bunch of wild concepts. Really good, really wild concepts.

On the drive home, I did a mental exercise focused entirely on how to get help. I knew what I didn't know—that was the easy part—I had no idea how to hire a head of sales. I started to go through a mental list of all the current or former CEOs I knew who had successfully done what I was trying to do.

Along the side of 101, I saw a billboard that reminded me of a former connection from my investment banking days. Mark Leslie, the wildly successful CEO of a software company called Veritas, had sold his company and now was teaching at the Stanford Business School. Recently, someone had emailed me one of his publications, which happened to be focused on hiring and building out a professional sales team.

*Well, holy shit! Mark might be a good person to talk to about my dilemma. Thanks, Coach,* I thought as a smile crossed my face. I didn't know the answer, but at least I had an idea of where to get some help.

The next day, I emailed Mark and asked if I could buy him breakfast and pick his brain about sales leadership and hiring for the sales function. Mark agreed to meet me and gave me some of the best professional advice I had ever received about how to think about the hiring process.

In retrospect, the first part of my process for seeking help was self-awareness. While I'm better at applying self-awareness on my own now, in this case, I was forced into it by circumstance. Firing my third VP of sales made the deficits obvious. This led me to Coach, whose advice led me to Mark. Self-awareness also allowed me to admit some of the simple mistakes I had made to Mark, so that I could get pointed and practical advice.

In finding the help I needed, I realized it wasn't reasonable to think I would magically know what to look for in a sales leader. I've never run a sales department. Beyond selling beer at Bengals games, I'd never even been a salesperson. Thankfully, Mark was willing to provide specific, actionable advice. This, in turn, helped me refine my process and find the perfect fit for our head of sales position.

All because Coach had convinced me to ask for help.

## QUIETING MR. MONKEY

As you reach out to peers and the leaders in your industry to ask for help, you'll see first-hand that other people have knowledge gaps, too. Every successful person can point to someone who helped them reach their desired result. Every single one. When you realize you're not alone in your struggles or your need for help, Mr. Monkey becomes less of an enemy. When you're not ashamed to ask for help, he has fewer sore spots to poke, and you can examine what he's saying in a different light.

After my meeting with Coach, I got in the car, and Mr. Monkey was waiting for me in the passenger seat.

*"Numbnut was being nice,"* he said, giving my shoulder a shove. *"I can't believe you just told Bill Fucking Campbell about your firing mistakes. He must think you're a complete*

*jackass. I told you that you don't know what you are doing—
and I was right."*

I shrugged. "Yeah. You were. It wasn't bad feedback."

He tried to play it cool, but I could see the shock on his face.
He'd been expecting an argument.

*"Yeah, well..."* he said, fiddling with the radio to change the
station. *"I know what I'm talking about."*

"Sometimes, you do." I changed the radio back to my station.
"But you really need to work on your delivery."

## THE EXTRA BONUS OF ASKING FOR HELP

In addition to getting the help you need, and gaining perspective from your peers, there's an added, less obvious benefit
to asking for help. Odd as it may sound, asking someone for
help endears you to the person you ask, because it builds the
helper's self-esteem and makes them feel useful. People like
helping. It makes them feel important, and who doesn't like
that? When you ask a friend or mentor for input and they give
you help, their accomplishment creates a feeling of euphoria
they will associate with you, creating a halo effect. So, even
though it may seem counterintuitive, numerous studies have
been done to prove that asking for help is one of the most effective ways to inspire positive feelings and build relationships.

Now when I have an issue to resolve, I typically ask four to five people for help. By asking for help, I'm frequently able to accelerate solutions and growth at levels I wouldn't have thought possible, and I'm strengthening my relationship with my network as well.

Being a great leader and entrepreneur takes courage, confidence, and the willingness to achieve what others have not been able to accomplish in the past. It also means knowing you're going to make a bunch of mistakes, and being more than just "okay" with it.

However, without self-awareness and a willingness to ask for help, I would wager that your chances of success are significantly lowered. Asking for help while you're striking out on your own as an entrepreneurial trailblazer might sound counterintuitive in some ways. The world likes to tell the story of entrepreneurs who have a "magic touch" that turns every idea to gold. But the reality is that everyone needs help, and you need to find the help that will move the needle most for you; I've given you a list of what worked for me in the Monkey Minders at the end of this chapter, but they aren't a definitive list. Learning how to get the help you need doesn't happen by checking off items someone else selected for you. Maybe the help you need comes through a collection of mentors, a good therapist, and cultivating a meditation practice. You might need an executive coach, planned time with friends, and a pet rabbit. Finding the help you need is part of your job as an entrepreneur, and learning to ask for it will bring you that much closer to authenticity—which is our next topic.

### MONKEY MINDERS #2: HOW TO GET SOME HELP

- *Prioritize your needs.* Figure out, right now, what you need the most help with on your entrepreneurial journey. Focus first on self-awareness to get an inventory of your strengths and weaknesses, as described in chapter three. Think about your most significant pain point and highest priority. Now you know where you need the most help. This is usually a relatively simple exercise, and it makes sense to do this often, as your answers will certainly change over time.

- *Find mentors who are relevant to your needs.* Coach was a firm believer in not just having one mentor but multiple mentors. You need someone who can help you with where you are at your current stage, and as your company grows, you will need a mentor familiar with that level of operation. You need someone who can help you think about what functional areas you're not good at, and someone who can help productively frame your role as CEO. When looking for a mentor, be conscious of accessibility and relatability. Often people looking for a mentor will seek out someone who is ridiculously busy or someone who ran a company twenty years ago and doesn't understand what's happening in the industry now. It's most important to find people who can relate directly to what you're doing at the moment.

- *Join a group.* Early in my journey, I was invited to join the local chapter of the Young Presidents' Association (YPO), which is like a support group of and for CEOs. Joining YPO had a massive impact on my career by helping me hone my job skills through sharing experiences and learning from other CEOs and entrepreneurs. YPO is one of several global organizations designed to help founders and CEOs. Others include Entrepreneurs Organization (EO), Vistage, and Chief Executive Network. No one ever perfects the craft of being an entrepreneur, and having access to people who understand the challenges you may be facing at every stage is a fantastic resource. The key is to find a group that works for you and provides you with opportunities to expand your perspective. If there isn't a chapter of YPO near you, or it's not quite the right fit, consider organizations like your local Rotary Club, small business association, or Chamber of Commerce. The key is to search for organizations in your specific field of business, online or locally. If the right group for you isn't out there, consider starting one yourself.

- *Get a professional coach.* For the longest time, I couldn't imagine why a founder or CEO would need a coach. It seemed like a sign of weakness. Boy, was I wrong. Inspired by Coach Bill, I found an executive coach who taught me how to be good at my job. I believe Coach's exact words were, "Steve Jobs needs a coach. Tiger Woods needs a coach. No offense, but why the hell doesn't Mike Smerklo have that kind of help?"

- *Get a dog.* Okay, maybe you don't have to get a dog specifically, but you do need a support network outside of work to give you the love and care you need to do your job and navigate all of the ups and downs that are coming your way. Help doesn't always have to be advice or mentorship. Sometimes it's nice just to have someone who loves you unconditionally, warts and all.

## ☞ CHAPTER FIVE ☜

# A–AUTHENTICITY

*"We shall not cease from exploration. And the end of all our exploring will be to arrive where we started. And know the place for the first time."*

—T.S. ELIOT

Authenticity is clearly one of the most important qualities in a leader. But a lot of the talk about authenticity in leadership makes it sound as if it's a simple choice to make—just *be authentic.* Well, if it were that simple, everyone would be. One look at the self-help shelf of any bookstore reveals that authenticity is something many people, not just entrepreneurs, seriously struggle to develop.

To do so, you have to lay the groundwork. If you don't know your strengths and weaknesses (S—Self), you will struggle to be an effective leader. If you don't have resources

(H—Help), it is damn near impossible to make improving yourself a priority.

The good news is that you can use self-awareness and coaching to take your entrepreneurial game to the next level, which allows you to begin showing up as an authentic leader. Once you've done the work to build yourself as an authentic leader, everything gets easier, because you'll find that you're able to check your problems against your core values to find solutions. Sounds great, right? Well, there is one catch...

OK, it isn't really a catch. More like a confession. I never felt truly comfortable as a leader and struggled with being an authentic one. I am not sure I ever got it close to right. I was good—maybe great—at letting my team know when I wasn't happy with a particular outcome. It would be more accurate to refer to this as "being an asshole."

At times, I was petty, self-serving, mean, and a downright shithead. But, like the proverbial bull in the china shop, I didn't realize I was the bull, and while I did hear glassware and fine china breaking all around me, I didn't exactly know the cause of the chaos. Eventually, I made progress through heavy coaching, but most of what I am going to share in this chapter is about what I saw other leaders do well. This is to say that most of the wisdom in this chapter about A-Authenticity comes from observation versus personal mastery.

**GREG REYES**

In 1999, I was twenty-nine years old, working in Silicon Valley as a junior investment banker at Morgan Stanley. It seemed like every company was going public. It was the height of the dot-com boom and technology stocks were soaring. The market was on fire. A stock valued at $10 might trade at $110 the next day. Companies could go public and be worth billions of dollars almost overnight.

When a company is about to go public, the CEO and key players from management and the investment bankers go on an IPO (Initial Public Offering) roadshow. The roadshow is a cross-country sales presentation for large investors. A roadshow will kick off in Boston or New York, holding meetings every hour from eight o'clock in the morning to five o'clock in the evening, telling the story of the company over and over. At the end of the day, the team gets back on the plane and flies to the next stop to do it again the next day. They'll hit every major city across the country over the course of the tour. As a junior investment banker, roadshow travel amounts to a grueling couple of weeks away from the office overseeing trip logistics and travel requests from the client while all your other work piles up on your desk.

Most of the bankers I worked with saw roadshows as something to endure, but I saw them as an opportunity. Sometimes, all of it was boring as shit. Most of the clients were nerdy technology people who would report back with a few benign requests: they'd appreciate a Starbucks coffee in the morning, they're allergic to dairy, or they'd prefer it if meetings didn't start prior to eight thirty in the morning. I worked hard to make it fascinating and used the time to my advantage. All the time I spent with company leaders in the backs of cabs racing to meetings and on long flights gave me a chance to ask them about their experiences. My secret power was being personable and getting them to tell me their stories. I learned something from every one of them.

In March of that year, I was assigned to work on the IPO roadshow for Brocade Communications. The CEO, Greg Reyes, was thirty-five years old. I didn't know Reyes that well, but from my few encounters with him, while prepping for the IPO, I knew this roadshow would be interesting.

Picture a young George Clooney playing a tech CEO, but add six inches and a hundred pounds of muscle, and you've got Greg Reyes. Reyes isn't an engineer; he's a salesperson by nature. He had been a college football player and was probably the most aggressive human I've ever met. At a time when Silicon Valley was rife with alpha males, Greg Reyes was alpha times a hundred, and for me, it was platonic love at first sight. When I met him, I thought, "Oh shit, this is the guy I want to be." He was a successful version of my Uncle Joe. Okay, a very, very successful version of my Uncle Joe.

The Brocade roadshow was set to start on a Sunday morning,

and on Friday afternoon, the expected "management request list" was emailed over to the roadshow support team and me. Reyes sent the craziest list of requests I'd ever seen:

- *Every time we're on the jet, I want twenty-four Heinekens on ice. Ice cold. No excuses.*
- *The banking team must have at least two extra cans of Copenhagen Smokeless Tobacco for me. I might run out or forget my tin. This is imperative.*
- *When the plane takes off, Apocalypse Now or The Thin Red Line will be playing on the media center. No exceptions please.*
- *Whenever the limo picks me up in the morning, The Howard Stern Show must be on the radio.*

It went on and on. They were mandates, not suggestions. This was back before streaming video, so over the weekend, I had to track down a store that carried DVD copies of the films he requested and also load up on tins of dip, per his request.

On Sunday, I was supposed to be on the private plane to prep before Reyes got there. We were scheduled to take off from San Jose Jet Center at one o'clock in the afternoon, but I was running late—a bad habit that I still carry with me to this day. I am always running late.

I didn't leave my house until twelve thirty in the afternoon, and then, tearing down the peninsula in my old Ford Explorer, I hit a slowdown on the 280. Mr. Monkey rode shotgun the entire time, berating me as I attempted to weave through traffic.

I sprinted to the runway, embarrassed and self-conscious. As I climbed the stairs to the plane, Warren Zevon's song "Excitable Boy" was blasting from the sound system. Not like kind of loud. Think eardrum-shattering loud.

"Goddammit, you're late, Smerklo. We almost left you!" Reyes shouted. He was already stretched out in one of the club chairs, Heineken in hand, a dip of Copenhagen across his whole bottom lip. "Sit your ass down and get a beer, goddammit!"

First thought: *Is he really drinking a beer and chewing tobacco at the same time?*

Second thought: *I'm either really going to like this guy, or he's going to kill me.*

It was clear, even then, that with Greg Reyes, there was no middle ground.

Over the weeks I spent with Reyes on the Brocade Roadshow, he became a role model for me. I hadn't had any role models growing up, other than sports coaches and Uncle Joe's best efforts. Reyes filled part of that missing father figure role in my life and gave me an example of what it meant to be a powerful, successful man. Today, Reyes's view of the world would be viewed as highly inappropriate. Be the man. Kill or be killed. Take no prisoners. He had an unrelenting bias for action and believed in never showing weakness. He also had an unusual counter to all that bluster. As big of an ass as he could be, he was also incredibly likable and charismatic to a fault. He was the first CEO who really talked with me about how he prepared himself for the job.

It was like getting running tips from an Olympic gold medal winner, and his coaching helped shaped my motivation into a specific plan. By the time the Brocade IPO was over, I knew it was time for me to get after my dreams. To get off the sidelines and start making the "work third" of my life matter. I was *going* to be an entrepreneur. Now all I had to do was make it happen.

The Brocade roadshow was a success. The stock had been priced at $10, but the first trade was at $33 and kept going up. Within a year, Reyes was worth several hundred million dollars.

Our relationship continued after the roadshow. I went fishing with Reyes. He took me on hunting trips. I started to study his habits and pick his brain. Eventually, he coached me in the skills I needed to obtain to be a successful entrepreneur and CEO.

"You know what your number-one issue is?" Reyes said one time between sips of Heineken as we hunted deer on his ranch a year after the IPO.

"What?"

"You wear your emotions on your face. I can always tell when you're mad or happy about something. If you want to be a CEO, you have to learn to have more of a poker face. You can't let people know what you're thinking."

Reyes could be rough. He was mean about the lessons he shared with me sometimes. But there was a lot of goodness in him, too; in many ways, he was an excellent mentor. Every time I called him with an issue, he would give me a big shove in the direction he thought was best. Reyes was the one who told me that I had to start truly believing in myself. He was the first person who took an interest in me and told me I could do this.

"Make it happen," he would always say. It was his go-to phrase. As I began to adopt it, I started to see how that bias toward action had power.

I started to put my plans of becoming an entrepreneur into action. I dreamed of being like Reyes. It felt odd and uncomfortable at first, but the image felt a lot better than thinking about good old Mr. Monkey. I knew that someday I would take my lessons from Reyes and emulate his persona as a leader. That vision and mindset seemed to quiet the hairy beast in my head just a little bit.

The only problem now, as Reyes so kindly pointed out as I shared my dreams with him, was that, well, I didn't have any good startup ideas, and I'd never really run anything close to a business. I'm sure he made fun of the shirt I was wearing as well, just to underscore his point.

But hey, good advice is good advice. I started to think about how I could get some experience in the near term before I went on to world domination, Reyes-style.

And that lead me to a fascinating breakfast meeting.

## BEN HOROWITZ

I knew right away that I didn't want to work for Ben Horowitz.

I arrived at LoudCloud's stealth office—a recently converted warehouse in Sunnyvale—early on a Saturday morning for my interview with the founders of what was being whispered about as the hottest start-up in Silicon Valley. This was 1999. It was peak dot-com startup craziness, and Ben Horowitz, the company's thirty-something CEO, was the talk of the town. I was beyond eager to meet him.

Silicon Valley culture was far from the business environment I'd grown accustomed to in investment banking. At Morgan Stanley, we'd made a move to a more casual office, but that meant instead of wearing tailored suits we opted for khakis, Brooks Brothers shirts, and Gucci loafers.

When I walked into the LoudCloud warehouse, my button-down shirt felt immediately out of place. The warehouse was in total disarray. Workspaces carved out of chaos. They operated at a whole different level of casual. I felt like Neo after taking the red pill in *The Matrix*. Suddenly, nothing seemed to make sense.

Ben stood up to greet me and offered the weakest handshake I had ever felt. If Reyes was the poster child for alpha male, Ben was central casting for an introverted, highly intelligent engineer. Soft-spoken and calm, Ben looked and acted much older than his actual age. He paid little attention to personal appearance and seemed apathetic to his CEO title and the power that went with it. I was quickly taken aback by the interview, largely because it was very clear that Ben Horowitz was basically the anti-Greg Reyes.

The interview went okay, but as I walked from Ben's office I was very, very confused.

Just a few days earlier, as 1999 was drawing to a close, I'd met with Marc Andreessen for breakfast at the Hobee's just off Highway 101. Marc had invented the first widely-used web browser, had founded Netscape, and had landed on the cover of Time Magazine by the time he was twenty-four. Wired magazine called him "The Man Who Makes the Future." Now he was starting another company, focusing on using business software on the network (now called the cloud).

Hyper-energetic and articulate, Marc is simply brilliant. During our short breakfast, I stopped trying to keep up with him and instead focused on not embarrassing myself. The meeting was supposed to be about helping him raise money, but near the end of the breakfast he simply said, "Hey, I've got a better idea. Why don't you come work for us?"

"Work for you, Marc?" I responded quickly, trying to play it as cool as possible, my head spinning with possibilities and opportunities.

"No. I'm a shitty manager. I am going to be chairman. I don't ever want to have any direct reports except the CEO. So you need to meet my co-founder, Ben. You will love Ben. He's going to be CEO and he is amazing. We're going to build a massive company."

Reyes had been encouraging me to gain operating experience with a move like this and Marc had proven success behind him. It seemed like the perfect opportunity, but when

I met Ben, I started to have doubts. He didn't carry himself the way I thought a CEO was supposed to.

*I'm not sure that's the guy I want to work for*, I thought, largely because I had put Reyes on such a high pedestal. When I expressed my doubts to Marc after the meeting with Ben, he reassured me.

"No, Ben's the real deal," Marc said, cocksure and concise as always. "This is great. You need to join us."

"Uh...okay," I muttered, quickly regaining my composure and smiling as Marc beamed at me, daring me not to accept the offer. "I'll do it. The only issue is that I have to wait a few weeks until I can start. My bonus from Morgan Stanley will get paid in mid-January, and I can start right after."

"Sure. Sounds great. See you then!" And Marc was gone, bounding off to his next interview.

A few weeks later, I would indeed quit my job at Morgan Stanley, painfully resisting the aforementioned offer to earn a million dollars for one year of work. I wanted to learn how to start a company. That urge to leap was like a flashing light telling me I was wired to be an entrepreneur. But I was still terrified. I understood that from the outside, this wasn't going to look like a sensible decision.

"You did what?" my mother said when I told her about my decision. Sitting back in Ohio, in front of her computer at eleven o'clock in the evening, I could almost hear her shaking her head. Never mincing her words, she followed her question with another question.

"Are you crazy? You could be shoveling shit in hell and still be happy, given how much money you're making right now!"

Truth be told, I had no idea what I was doing other than following some gut instinct. *Is this the right move?* I thought. *Am I crazy?*

I did it anyway because it felt like the next step to becoming an entrepreneur. I went to work for LoudCloud in January of 2000.

## IT'S ALL ABOUT THE BENJAMINS

In February, I had the first chance to hear Ben speak to a large group. At the first all-hands meeting, Ben got on the makeshift stage in his ill-fitting jeans and t-shirt to address the group of twenty employees and started quoting rap lyrics. My memory is a bit hazy, but I think he started with P Diddy's "It's All About the Benjamins."

Ben used the lyrics of the song to illustrate salient management principles and why the focus on making money is essential.

I knew rap from the blaring boom boxes at the inner-city basketball courts in Toledo. I would go most summer nights back in high school to play against the best athletes in town. The other players always called me "Bird," as in Larry Bird. Not because I was good, but because I was the only white person in the entire park. I fell in love with rap back in the mid-80s. The ethos of hustle, the bravado and ambition, and the "do or die" lyrics resonated with me like nothing else.

What was this dude, Ben Horowitz, doing quoting rap lyrics? It didn't feel right—so out of place on that small makeshift stage in Sunnyvale, California, and in a business setting in general. I looked around, expecting the people around me to share in the awkwardness of the moment, but the engineers were blown away. Ben was being real. He wasn't using buzzwords. They loved the guy. Later, I learned that Ben had actually written and produced his own rap songs when he was a kid, so quoting Diddy wasn't a façade, but a thoughtful way of expressing himself. But at the time, it all felt surreal and out of place.

I turned to my friend and colleague Pete Gifford and we both stared each other wide-eyed. I had recruited Pete from Morgan Stanley and he had made a similar sacrifice to join me on this journey. Blond-haired, blue-eyed, and typically calm and unflappable, Pete's comments said it all.

"Are we on fucking *Mars?*"

Neither of us dared to try and answer that question. We didn't really want to know the answer.

For the next two years, I struggled with Ben. He was not like me, and he wasn't what I imagined a leader should be. He's not salesy or gregarious. He doesn't have a lot of the attributes of physical presence I'd been conditioned to admire. In my mind, a true leader showed up dressing the part, showing strength, and conveying confidence.

Ben may not have looked like a leader to me, but his speaking ability and the way he communicated with his employees made people want to follow him to the ends of the earth. Ben was the anti-Reyes, but he was just as powerful in his own way.

I don't think Ben is ever not authentic. It's impossible for him to bullshit. He has to tell the truth. If someone had a dumb idea, Ben would say, "That's a really dumb idea." It would be uncomfortable and awkward, but it was what he believed. When Ben criticized someone's idea, there was no venom behind it. Ben was just expressing himself. If he thought your idea was bad, and he told you, it was unsettling at first, but the consistency of Ben's behavior is his superpower. Once you get used to it, you know that he doesn't hold anger over a dumb idea, and by pointing out the flaws of a plan, he's creating the chance to get to a better idea.

After less than two years, I quit my job at LoudCloud. The company had gone public, but the stock wasn't doing well. I was frustrated with Ben and Marc.

*These guys are lunatics,* I thought as I left the company. *They don't know what they're doing.* All the other times I'd left a company I'd done well maintaining ties, but not in this case. I did not leave smoothly. As my lifelong friend Shawn O'Neill likes to point out, I ran across that bridge with a blowtorch tied to my ass. I'd left such a huge salary to join this startup, and the lack of reward had tempered my feelings toward the company. I started the job dreaming of the mansion on the hill I was going to buy with my stock-option wealth. I left with enough money to buy a new mountain bike. I was bitter. I was about to turn thirty-two years old and felt like my clock was ticking. If I didn't move soon and get after my own entrepreneurial journey, it would be too late.

It's hard to imagine what being an entrepreneur is like until you do it yourself. Reyes gave me tips before I was in the game. I didn't know it at the time, but watching Ben and Marc operate a startup during the dot-com bust was like being in Kenya, training every day with sub-two-hour marathon runners. It was all on, all the time. I just wished I would have said *thank you* at the time. Remember early in the book when I talked about ways to figure out that *you might be an entrepreneur?*

I guess you can add arrogance to the list as well.

## DO YOU FIRE THE MASCOT?

Four years after buying ServiceSource, the company had grown to several hundred employees. We had wisely hired an executive, Ray Martinelli, as our first head of Human Resources to help us manage the expanding enterprise. Balanced and thoughtful, Ray was a trusted advisor who always focused on how every business decision we made would affect our employees. He had significant impact on the business and continued to bring new frameworks and processes to the organization. One of the ideas Ray brought forward was a data-driven approach to reviewing employees and determining their potential within the company.

One late fall day, Ray presented the results from his deep and extensive analysis of each and every employee. Ray shared a PowerPoint filled with assessments of employee performance and potential at our annual planning and budgeting session. I sat there watching, affecting my best Reyes stance. I put a dip of tobacco in my lower lip, leaned back in my chair and casually lifted my feet up to rest on the conference table.

Ray showed the entire executive team a grid of high-performing, high-potential employees we'd obviously want to keep. Then he moved on to employees who had low potential but performed well at their current job level, and employees who had great potential, but weren't performing well in their current job and needed to be moved to a different position.

Then Ray continued to the low-potential employees who weren't doing well at their jobs.

*Well, this isn't going to be easy,* I thought. *But this is what a real CEO does.* I knew it was my job to make tough personnel decisions. I took my feet off the table, leaned forward, and rested my chin on my folded hands. *Time to switch from casual observer to focused leader,* I thought, projecting my best alpha-male casual confidence while Ray continued with his presentation.

As Ray began to populate his PowerPoint screen with low-performing, low-potential employee names, one of the first names he added was Jack Donatello.*

My heart fell.

When David and I first bought ServiceSource and met all the employees, a man approached to shake our hands.

"Hi, my name is Donno," he said. "Jack Donatello, but everyone calls me Donno. I was the first employee hired here, and I love this company. I love the culture, and I'm so passionate about what we're doing. I want you to know that whatever you guys are thinking about for the future, I'm here for the long haul."

I could tell right away that Donno was a character. A good

one. I instantly liked him. I remember sharing with him that everyone outside of my professional network called me Smerk, and that I was pretty sure that most of my high school and college friends might struggle to recall my first name. He understood.

Donno didn't have any specific specialty in the company, but we would move him from one department to another. He was always on board to do whatever we thought was best for the team. He was the guy at company happy hours full of energy and telling stories.

At one company Christmas party, I saw him sitting with a key employee talking solemnly. I had no idea what they were discussing.

A few days later, our HR representative came over and said, "Hey, Nate was planning to quit, but luckily, Donno, I mean Jack, spent an hour and a half with him at the Christmas party and talked him out of it."

Donno was the lifeblood of the company. He kept everyone connected to the roots of ServiceSource, sharing stories about the early days when the company started out in an old purple building off Lombard Street. He took my vision for the culture of the company, became part of it, and found a way to amplify those values. But as the company grew from thirty, to ninety, to hundreds of employees, everyone's roles grew more specialized, and it became apparent that Donno was a jack-of-all-trades and a master of none.

When Donno's name appeared on Ray's PowerPoint slide, I heard everyone around me sigh and grumble.

"Oh, crap! Donno?"

"Shit, man! Not Donno!"

Kevin Maddock was our executive vice president of inside sales, and the bulk of our employees reported to him. Kevin was always equitable and unshakable, the opposite of me. Kevin cleared his throat and said, "It's going to be a challenging move, but I think it's the right thing to do. As Mike always says, there's no room for mascots."

Katy Keim, my head of marketing, turned toward me slowly. A fellow Midwesterner, Katy is 5'3" of intense energy. She was usually the first of the group to share her point of view. In this moment, she was quiet, but the look on her face said it all. *Are you really this big of an asshole, Mike?* I looked away quickly.

Everyone was waiting for my response. I could feel my pulse speed up. Sweat beaded on my upper lip. And there was Mr. Monkey, staring at me from across the conference room.

*"Do you want to be admired or feared, Mike?"* Mr. Monkey said, a bulge of dip in his bottom lip. *"Fuck this guy. He can't hack it. Too bad! He's out."*

The hairy bastard stared at me with scorn and disdain. I leaned against the conference table and shook my head, trying to buy myself a moment to think.

Mr. Monkey was saying all the things I knew Reyes would say if I called to ask him for advice.

*"Why are we even talking about this? Are you getting soft now? Are you a wimp? Why are you even wasting time pausing on this? There's no reason not to fire a low-potential low performer."*

But at this moment I realized that I wasn't Greg Reyes. I thought about the moment in *Wall Street* where Charlie Sheen's character stands up to Gordon Gekko, saying that as much as he wanted to be Gordon, he wasn't. I thought I wanted to be Reyes, but at my core, I simply wasn't that much like him. I imagined what Ben would do and quickly realized how blunt and specific he would be in this moment. But that wasn't me either. I really didn't know what to do or who to emulate. Mr. Monkey, Reyes, and Ben all seemed to swim in my head simultaneously, each shouting at me to listen to their point of view.

I also realized that I didn't know the right answer, and suddenly felt okay with it. I did something very unusual for me at the time. I simply turned to my team and said quietly, "You know, I really don't know what to do here, and I could use some help".

*"What did you just say?"* I could hear Mr. Monkey screaming in my ear. *"You don't know what to do and you need help. Good God, Mike, have you lost your mind?"*

As the faces around the table softened, I knew it was critical to ignore the monkey's blabbering once again. For the next few hours, I watched as my team worked together on a solution. We talked about the type of company we wanted to build and the culture we wanted to operate in. We went back to look at Donno's potential and uncover what we'd missed in the evaluation. I think someone referenced the mattress story. We even changed one of our core values from "win" to "win as a team."

Donno stayed with ServiceSource long after I left. We moved him around to several different roles, and he thrived in each one. He helped us open some of our international offices and manage new sales engagements. Overall, we started to look at employees differently, by putting culture forward as one of our priorities when we measured potential, placing value on an employee's ability to amplify culture.

And I found my voice of authenticity, somewhere between

the confidence of Reyes and directness of Horowitz, and with a sprinkle of vulnerability that drove Mr. Monkey nuts. It wasn't checkmate in my chess match with Mr. Monkey, not by a long shot. But it sure felt like progress.

## WHO THE HELL ARE YOU?

Being an entrepreneur starts out hard, and it never gets easier. This is partly due to the fact that the job is always changing. No two days are alike, and most of the time you have to make real-time decisions with limited information. Plus, most entrepreneurs are first-timers, learning leadership on the fly as well.

Early on, I felt like a "play actor"—imagining what I thought other, more successful CEOs would do if they were in my shoes. It wasn't until I was faced with a seemingly small decision about a mid-level employee that I finally recognized what my job as an entrepreneur and leader was all about: to authentically pursue the vision and direction that I believed was best for the good of the entire organization.

I realize now that much of what I learned came from a wide array of mentors, but the contrast between Ben and Reyes has always amused me. It took me too long to find the balance between the two, but eventually, I did, and learned to be comfortable with that tension. As an entrepreneur, you need mentors and role models to help and guide you. But authenticity only happens when you stop playing the part and find your own voice. Like every concept in this formula, finding this voice is easy to understand but hard to put in practice.

Like I pointed out earlier, dozens, if not hundreds, of books have been written about authentic leadership, so obviously there is no one true answer. But that's the point, isn't it? It's up to *you* to find your authentic voice; no one can give you a script. I see a lot of entrepreneurs trying to "act the part." I did it for quite a while. It's exhausting, and it doesn't work. The key is to take the time and figure out how you want to show up as a leader, get comfortable with it, and take it from there. In the Monkey Minders at the end of this chapter, I've laid out some simple ideas to help.

Authenticity is certainly going to help you show up as an effective leader and deal with all the inevitable challenges you will face along your journey. The good—or bad—news? Entrepreneurs never run out of challenges. And without persistence, our next topic, your entrepreneurial journey will be a very short one.

## MONKEY MINDERS #3: HOW TO FIND YOUR AUTHENTIC VOICE

- *Get curious about your voice.* There are countless sources of deep insights that will dramatically extend the concept of authentic leadership beyond the highlights of this chapter. Some of my favorite books on the subject include *The Hard Thing about the Hard Thing*, by Ben Horowitz, which tells the story of Loudcloud/Opsware, Clay Christopher's *How Will You Measure Your Life*, and Howard Schultz's *Pour Your Heart into It*. There are so many resources from which to choose. The key is to listen to what others have done and also begin to think about how you want to show up as a leader and entrepreneur.

- *(S) + (H) → (A).* Make a list of settings where you feel most comfortable as a leader. When are you in your "zone of genius?" Then list when you are least comfortable. This list will help you gain insight into when you're able to most easily display authentic leadership, and when you might struggle. For me, sitting around talking financial analysis or brainstorming about strategy feels very comfortable, and it's easy for the most authentic version of myself to shine through. However, I have never been good at giving direct criticism or managing confrontation calmly, so it is very easy for me to get out of authentic mode when dealing with these situations.

- *Role models.* Write down the list of the role models you most want to emulate as a leader and entrepreneur. Now take a closer look at what you find so appealing about these role models. Do you see them as authentic, or do you suspect they're hiding their insecurity? I was insecure as a leader and therefore used a role model I thought of as the opposite of me in an attempt to cover this up. My strategy worked in the short term but not the long term, and eventually prevented me from being myself. To uncover my authentic self, I had to examine who I was emulating and why—and make sure my role models were consistent with how I wanted to show up as an entrepreneur.

- *Musts versus nice-to-have(s)*. Make a list of what you would consider as "must-have" versus "nice-to-have" attributes of authentic leadership as they relate to your long-term goals. What would you sacrifice, and what would you never consider as you clear the path toward your dream? What do you value most? What behaviors and choices are unacceptable? Assuming all legal, ethical, and moral considerations are a given, realize that there is no wrong answer. The purpose of this exercise is to find your personal "true north." What do you want the company you started to stand for? The very best entrepreneurs in the Next Coast Ventures portfolio have all clearly defined their true north from the start and never waver from that particular navigation. It shows in both the performance of the company and the culture of the organization.

# CHAPTER SIX

# P–PERSISTENCE

*"What? Over? Did you say 'over'? Nothing is over until we decide it is! Was it over when the Germans bombed Pearl Harbor? Hell no!"*

—BLUTO, *ANIMAL HOUSE*

For starters, I want to emphasize that this part—**P**—is my favorite aspect of the SHAPE methodology. All the other elements of the formula, **S, H, A,** and **E,** were things I employed inconsistently at best during my entrepreneurial days. The advice that I share in the other parts of the SHAPE Mindset is largely a result of what I have learned from other entrepreneurs. But not persistence.

As an entrepreneur, I raised a lot of money from investors. I had a go-to ending to my fundraising presentations: after ending the formal business summary, I would slowly shut my laptop and look around the room, making eye contact with each of the potential investors. Taking a deep breath, I would make a simple statement: "This is either going to be a massive success, or you can pry my dead body out of my office." The group would laugh nervously, but I wouldn't let up on my stare.

Years later, an investor who backed me recalled the story and noted that after the meeting, his partners in the firm didn't know if I was joking or not. Truth be told, neither did I.

## THE SUN SHINES ON THE SAINT AND THE SINNER ALIKE

Seven years into my journey as an entrepreneur, the small business I bought in 2003 now had several hundred employees around the world and was firing on all cylinders. In 2010, the company was highlighted in the San Francisco Business Journal when we reached $100 million in revenue. The future looked bright for the business, and I was becoming more comfortable in my own skin, both personally and professionally.

In 2008, David had a health issue that forced him to step away from the day-to-day operations of the business. Fortunately, he was okay, but it was a big loss for me and the company. The only upside was that it forced me to focus on building out a strong executive team—recruiting and hiring great leaders that brought deep expertise to each of our key functional areas. I struggled to give up my "command and control" management style, but having true experts on my team made it feel like the weight of the company no longer rested entirely on my shoulders.

My missteps in sales—including hiring a coke addict—were finally solved when I found an unconventional leader named Matt Rosenberg. Matt was leading our sales department, and he was thriving. Funny and unassuming, Matt operates like a wolf in sheep's clothing. Prospects never saw him coming and he was able to close huge deals without employing typical alpha-male tactics.

I also recruited an amazing right-hand person, Natalie McCullough, to help me in all aspects of the business. Natalie is wicked smart, intense, and focused—a real ass-kicker. Her sense of pragmatism was the perfect balance to my optimism and disdain for details. We worked hand in glove to turn a bunch of ideas into specific, measurable outcomes.

The "win as a team" value that we had developed after the Donno incident was more than some words on a poster hanging in a conference room. We embraced the concept across the company.

Sometimes, I actually felt like I knew what the hell I was doing.

There was only one real problem with the business. Sun Microsystems was our largest customer and made up 35 percent of our $100 million in annual revenue. Business books call this "customer concentration." In real life, it means you ignore your wife and kids trying to make sure this one customer loves you more than anything else in the world.

"What are you thinking about, Mike?" my wife would ask me at the end of a long day.

"Oh, nothing..." I'd murmur. Sure—nothing except *what the hell are we going to do if Sun cancels our contract?*

This level of customer concentration is scary for any company, but there was one additional wrinkle. Recently, my team and I had decided—over several bottles of wine at a leadership off site—that the time was right to take the company public. The idea of an IPO was hard to get my head around. Ten years prior, I had been the junior banker helping entrepreneurs take their company public. Twenty years ago, I had been selling beer at pro football games and didn't even know what an IPO was.

Was this really my professional life now?

My personal life had grown as well. Abby and I were married in 2005 and were blessed with three boys under the age of two: an eighteen-month-old, and nine-month-old twins. We'd just bought a five-bedroom house in Hillsborough; a beautiful, tree-lined suburban town mid-way down the San Francisco Peninsula. Our house bustled with cribs, baby toys, and chaos. The stress of work quickly faded when I walked into the house to see Abby, the boys, and our aging but ever-goofy chocolate Labrador Retriever, Miracle.

Was this really my personal life now?

*"This can't last. This can't last,"* Mr. Monkey liked to whisper in my ear.

"Actually, I think it will," I told him, trying to believe my own words. "We're doing all the right things. I am not alone in this journey anymore. I have a team at work and a family at home. This isn't a flash in the pan."

In reality, I fought hard to fend off my imposter syndrome and old self-destructive tendencies. The monkey seemed to keep getting better at his job as well. Had that bastard gotten himself an executive coach as well?

## APRIL 20, 2009

Just another Monday. I got out of bed at five-thirty in the morning, made coffee, and then snuck off to the small spare bedroom that served as my home office. I'd check the web for relevant industry news and answer e-mails until a quarter past six o'clock in the morning. Then I'd go for a run, be back home to shower, spend a few minutes with the boys before leaving for work around eight o'clock. That was my plan....

As I carried my mug of coffee to my desk, my cell phone immediately started buzzing. Nine text messages and a couple of missed voicemails. Something must be wrong. I glanced at the Technology Section on my Yahoo! newsfeed. The lead headline said it all: *Oracle to Acquire Sun Microsystems.*

Oracle, a dominant software company focused on database technology, had been on a buying spree for the past several years, focusing on legacy software companies with properties to add to its suite of products. Oracle had already bought a few of our previous customers. Each time, those customers terminated their relationship with us almost immediately as Oracle had a very clear and well-defined policy not to work with external vendors like ServiceSource. I dropped my head in my hands, trying not to hyperventilate. We knew that Sun was up for sale, but the company was primarily a hardware company—a segment of the technology landscape that had been historically off-limits for Oracle's acquisition spree.

Until today.

Oracle buying Sun was our doomsday scenario. I looked around the small office and then dropped my head into my hands in utter shock. This was beyond bad. As I scrolled through my texts, every single message was about Oracle.

Our Chief Customer Officer Jay Ackerman's simple text needed no explanation. "FUCK. FUCK. FUCK!"

That was all it needed to say. This turn of events left me, and ServiceSource, fucked. Not just capital "F" fucked. More like ALL CAPS FUCKED.

There were several more from board members saying, "Just saw the news. What does this mean for us?"

By the time I opened my e-mail, there were ten messages from colleagues who had seen the story and sent it along. Everyone on my executive team knew that this was the one "doomsday event" that could ruin the business, and here it was, happening.

Mr. Monkey got right in my face, shouting, *"Mike, I told you it wouldn't last. I told you this was a flash in the pan. I knew it was too good to be true."*

In the past, I might have responded frantically, firing off e-mails, and making angry phone calls to my team. Insecurity immediately overcame me, and anger—my go-to release valve—bubbled up in my veins. I tried to calm down and assess my alternatives. Shot of whiskey? Fortunately, it was six o'clock in the morning, so I quickly ruled out drinking as an option. I took some deep breaths and tried to think.

*"You're going to have to scramble and sell this company before disaster hits,"* Mr. Monkey said. *"Before you lose everything. Come on, Mike. Don't be weak. What are you going to do? What are you doing, Mike?"*

I shut my laptop.

"Well," I told Mr. Monkey, "first, I need to go for a run."

Mr. Monkey shook his head in disbelief as I put on my running shoes.

*"I knew this would happen,"* Mr. Monkey said. *"When you bought the company. When you bought this house. Last night, when you were playing with the kids, and feeling so happy and secure. I just knew it was all going to fall apart."*

I wanted to crawl in bed, or go to a bar—find escape in some way, shape, or form—but instead, I walked to the end of our driveway and ran down the hill. My limbs felt slow and heavy. I made it maybe a half a mile. I couldn't run any further. The moment of despair hit hard. I had no energy. I tried to push myself. "Power through" had always been my mantra, but I simply could not muster any strength.

The dreams and plans I'd had seemed to be flying out the window. Thirty-five percent of our revenue would go away almost overnight, and I was certain the idea of going public, and maybe even the hope of retaining any value as a company, and any job security for my employees was now in question. When your business has one large customer, it is like being hooked on a drug. We knew we should taper our "habit," but now it was too late. Like a junkie thrown into prison, cold turkey was the new reality.

I thought of all the people who'd had faith in me and my vision for this company, who'd put their time and resources into ServiceSource because I'd convinced them to believe in what we were trying to build.

"Damn," I muttered to myself. "I've worked so hard. I've pushed the rock uphill. Now this—what the hell are we going to do?" I couldn't run anymore.

So instead, I walked.

I began to cry slightly as I trudged several miles through a thick fog. It was a cool spring morning and the trees were just starting to bloom. The crisp morning air slowly gave way to the radiant sunshine. About a mile in, I tied my fleece around my waist. I could feel the sun's warmth on my arms. I took a moment to let my mind refresh.

*Okay, well, I'm alive*, I thought. *But, shit, what am I going to do?*

I walked back home. Abby was standing in front of three high chairs, spoon feeding each of the boys one by one, Miracle hovering nearby waiting for the inevitable Cheerio to fall. She could tell from the look on my face that something was wrong. The chaos of the moment helped me regain some perspective.

As I walked from the kitchen into my home office, I tried to come up with a plan of action.

Mr. Monkey was sitting at my desk, holding up my IPO preparation documents. *"Bet you don't need these anymore, huh, champ?"* he said, ripping the pages to shreds in front of me.

As I stood there, trying to gather the strength to call in to the office, I felt like Mr. Monkey was growing exponentially by the moment. He wasn't even a monkey anymore. He had grown to full King Kong gorilla size, taking up the entire office.

"Okay, okay," I said to myself. "This is not the time to go with your gut. Time to think."

I have always prided myself on my work ethic, persistence,

and general optimism when facing a challenge. But I knew that previous manifestations of persistence would not work this time. "Make it happen." "Power through it." "Work harder." "Die trying." All of those mantras had served me so well in the past, but not this time. I needed help.

My first call was to Bruce Dunlevie, my most experienced and balanced board member. Bruce is the founder of Benchmark, the legendary venture capital firm that had invested in ServiceSource several years earlier. Hyper-intelligent but thoughtful and balanced, Bruce has worked with the most prominent startups in Silicon Valley and experienced countless situations like this one.

"We will get through this, Mike. Stay calm and be open-minded." Calm, cool, and collected as always, Bruce's words brought my heart rate down considerably.

My next call was to Jim Ellis, another board member who had backed me from day one. A hugely successful entrepreneur, Jim's quick wit is matched only by his pragmatic problem-solving skills. Jim knew the drill and was immensely helpful about contingency planning and moving fast.

"Maybe you should try and isolate the issue. Don't get everyone spun up out of control, if possible. Kind of like a SWAT approach when negotiating with a terrorist, you know?"

Jim's idea seemed goofy, but I needed all the help I could get. I jotted down notes feverishly.

## ALL HANDS

At four o'clock that afternoon, I assembled all of the company's employees together. Standing in front of all of my coworkers, I struggled to find my bearings amid another flash of panic. I worried we would have to lay people off and start dramatically cutting expenses. Everyone in the audience wanted assurance. *Do you want to know everything is going to be okay or do you want the truth?* I thought to myself as I began my speech.

I used one of Ben Horowtiz's old tricks to start the meeting: I quoted rap lyrics from my favorite Public Enemy song, "He Got Game." The lyrics underscore how a champion never lets a win get to their head, or a loss hurt their heart.

"This may be a strange thing to say, but as a company, we've always been very good at not letting a win go to our heads. We've tried not to get cocky. We've tried never to get too full of ourselves. Now, we need to keep this loss from hurting our hearts. We need to recognize this as a real loss. We need to mourn this. That's all we're going to say today. Go home. Don't worry about it. I don't know how we're going to solve this yet and it's not what we've planned, but we still have a lot of resources. The executive team is going to spend the next couple of days thinking about it, and we'll come back to the employee base to fill everyone in."

Then I continued, "I think this may end up being the greatest thing that ever happened to the business. I know that sounds weird, but I think it is." I quietly closed out the meeting and desperately wondered how the hell this might actually be the case. The truth was, I had no idea how.

## THE PLAN

In the week after our Oracle doomsday, we developed a plan based on the "goofy" idea that Jim had provided me in our brainstorming session. We knew it was unlikely we could save Sun as a customer but we wanted to mitigate that loss for as long as possible. We also didn't want to have the entire company distracted by this effort so we set up a SWAT team, just like Jim had recommended. The SWAT team was led by Jay Ackerman, our chief customer officer. A former college hockey player, Jay is as competitive and focused as they come, and I freed him up to work to do everything he could to try and save Sun as a customer.

We told everyone else in the company to assume these efforts were a lost cause and begin to plan as if Sun were going away immediately. It seemed insane at first, but the strategy allowed the rest of the company to focus efforts toward ramping up sales and getting on with the business under this new reality. To go cold turkey, so to speak.

We tried everything we could to save Sun as a customer but to no avail. It was a rough year, full of sleepless nights and moments of sheer panic. It felt like we were on a plane headed toward a mountain range, and I feared we wouldn't have enough gas to make it over the crest and land safely in a field. I'd be lying if I said I didn't wake up in the middle of many nights in a cold sweat worried we'd crash into the rock face. However, we did recover. We figured out how to extend our contract to keep Sun as a customer for several months and used that time like fuel in our tank to carry us. We worked like hell to find new sources of revenue and ended up with a more balanced customer base. Oddly enough, this near death experience forced us to innovate, evolve our strategy, and move forward.

The off-handed, wishful remark I had made at the all-hands meeting turned out to be correct: the *worst* thing had actually turned out to be *best* thing. Persistence had paid off. The team came together on April 20, 2009, and solved what appeared at the time to be an impossible problem. That same team would gather in New York City, sipping champagne and celebrating when ServiceSource went public on March 24, 2011.

The German philosopher Friedrich Nietzsche said, "That

which does not kill us, makes us stronger." Turns out you have to pretty close to death to fully appreciate the power of that statement.

## THE SUN DOES INDEED SHINE ON EVERY ENTREPRENEUR

In retrospect, this story doesn't sound that bad, does it? Time has a tendency to soften the emotions.

My intention in telling the story wasn't to make you say, "Wow, what an amazing entrepreneur Mike was back in the day" (by now you know that would be a short blog post at best). My intention was to show you that every single entrepreneur has had at least one gut-wrenching "how are we going to survive" experience like I just described. Every entrepreneur has been up tossing and turning at four o'clock in the morning wondering, *What the hell are we going to do?*

You will start your business, get excited about the potential, and begin your journey as an entrepreneur—ready to take on the world. Then the dot-com bubble will burst. Or the tragedy of 9/11. Perhaps the financial crisis of 2007–2008. Who would ever plan for a global pandemic like the COVID-19 virus that is ravishing entrepreneurial dreams as I type this sentence? You don't know what will happen, but eventually the proverbial shit hits the proverbial fan.

If you want to be an entrepreneur, you, too, will have several of these moments. In fact, if you only have one or two "oh shit" moments as an entrepreneur, you will be incredibly lucky—most of us have had more than we care to recall or count.

Per usual, it won't matter what you ate for breakfast, how you structured your morning routine or any other bullshit "hack" that you read about before you decided to jump into the pool of entrepreneurship, naked and alone. The water will engulf you quickly and it will be really, really cold.

Of course, your dear friend Mr. Monkey will be there to offer all sorts of "advice." The real challenge is not to listen to him. The one thing you can control is between your ears. Your mindset and mental tenacity—your persistence—will be the only thing to keep you afloat.

## PERSISTENTLY PERSISTENT GLASS EATERS

At Next Coast Ventures, we developed a term for the type of entrepreneur we like to back. Tom Ball, my co-founder in the firm, is an amazing balance of intellect, street smarts, and scrappiness. An accomplished entrepreneur with a great sense of humor, Tom has also been through the ups and downs that go with the territory. Before we started the firm, we wrote down what we wanted the culture of the firm to be and what type of entrepreneurs we hoped to attract and invest behind. We pondered words like tenacious, ethical, fearless, focused, and committed.

But we chose the term "glass-eater" to describe the entrepreneurs that we get the most excited about and the ones we like to back the most.

Why this term? Well, it sums up what it takes to be successful. Imagine how painful and uncomfortable it would be to actually consume even a small quantity of glass. Not fun. Not playful. Not even close to enjoyable. But if you are willing to do it, you end up in a special class of humans.

You have a vision. You summon the courage to go after it. You deal with amazing ups and downs. Along the way something bad will happen that will shake you to the core. Imagine that, to survive it, you will have to eat some glass. You struggle but you make it happen. This term isn't meant to glorify struggle and suffering. Rather, it is a realistic view about how damn hard it is to start, grow, and run a business.

Glass-eating isn't fun, and it isn't for everyone. At Next Coast, we try and offer all the mustard and ketchup when we can—but we know success or failure depends on the entrepreneur. Glass might be all there is to eat for a while, but those who are persistent live to see another day. These are the real champions, and the reward is theirs and theirs alone. They make it happen, glass and all.

The biggest mistake you can make is to assume entrepreneurship is going to be easy. The short-form blog posts you might have gobbled up in the past are especially dangerous because they skip over all the hard parts of the journey. Entrepreneurship is a marathon, not a short sprint. A persistent mindset will help you have the endurance when you need it most and keep Mr. Monkey quiet while you power on. If you expect that there will be rough sailing ahead, you can mentally plan and prepare for the time when the storm hits your boat—and that's the topic of our next chapter.

## MONKEY MINDERS #4: HOW TO STAY PERSISTENT NO MATTER WHAT

- *Meditation.* Unfortunately for the leaders that worked for me, I didn't pick up this habit until after my time as a CEO. Sorry about that, team! Most of the most balanced and consistent entrepreneurs I know spend at least ten to fifteen minutes a day with some form of meditative practice. This sacred space provides time to reflect and helps the mind stay calm, balanced, and present regardless of the chaos that is unfolding. How you get this headspace doesn't matter, but a consistent practice will make a huge difference.

- *Read books about entrepreneurship.* Avoid short-form content—blog posts, podcasts, magazine articles— that don't take enough time to tell the whole story, with all the potential ups and downs. Courage and understanding is better sparked by long-form content like *Shoe Dog* (Phil Knight/Nike) that takes the time to detail the full journey of building a business. The expansive picture will help with motivation and enable you to fully grasp what persistence is all about.

- *Set long-term goals and dream big.* Taking the long view of your journey will help make the ups and downs seem less daunting. Keeping your big dreams in mind will help remind you why you jumped into this damn pool in the first place. During my entrepreneurial journey, I kept two quotes on my desk—hidden so that only I could see them. "Make sure you set goals so high that you can't possibly achieve them all in one lifetime. That way you will always have something ahead of you." (Ted Turner). "Make no small plans for they have no power to stir the soul." (Niccolo Machiavelli). Both of these kept me focused on the long haul, even in the worst moments.

- *Keep it all in perspective.* A particularly strong founder in the Next Coast Ventures portfolio refuses to make any business analogy that compares business with war or implies life or death. Regardless of how serious an issue appears, she knows that it isn't life or death. Yes, she has a big dream, and she is spending a massive amount of time and energy to make it successful, but she also has a grounded perspective on what is and what isn't at stake. If her company fails to meet its annual goals, no one is going to starve or die (fortunately). This discipline helps keep everyone balanced and puts all of the daily ups and downs that come with entrepreneurship in perspective.

- *Find an outlet outside of the office.* For me, a daily workout or time in nature did so much to rejuvenate my mind and body. Another one of the entrepreneurs in the Next Coast family shuts off his phone every night from six o'clock to eight o'clock in the evening in order to spend time with his family and remain present and attentive. At times, he will send me an email at ten o'clock in the evening after his family has gone to bed, but he won't sacrifice his special time each and every day. His productivity level is one of the highest I have ever seen. Everyone needs some balance and an outlet from the stress and strain of being an entrepreneur, but no one size fits all. The key is to find the right outlet for you and to guard it with extreme prejudice.

# CHAPTER SEVEN

# E-EXPECTATIONS

*"I know not all that may be coming, but be it what it will, I'll go to it laughing."*

—HERMAN MELVILLE, *MOBY-DICK*

Just like every story, your journey as an entrepreneur will have a beginning, a middle, and an end. Every day, week, month, and year will be different. There will be ups and downs. Some days, you will feel like the champion of the world. Other days, you'll wish you could hide in bed curled up in a ball with the covers pulled over your head. It doesn't matter if you're running a one-person show or overseeing a 1,000-person organization—your "job" will change constantly. The only certainty is that you will never be bored. But who wants a boring life, right?

Ironically, the constant state of flux during your entrepreneurial journey is what makes managing your expectations so difficult. That is why **E**xpectations comes last in the formula. Each step of your journey brings about changes, surprises, and unforeseen challenges. Nothing is ever constant or static. So with each new chapter your expectations will change and the real key is to reexamine them on a regular basis. The final piece in the puzzle to managing Mr. Monkey is all about expectations.

## IN THE BEGINNING

Marcus Aurelius, the Stoic philosopher, said, "When you wake up in the morning, tell yourself: the people I deal with today will be meddling, ungrateful, arrogant, dishonest, jealous, and surly."

Sounds like he and Mr. Monkey would enjoy hanging out together, huh? I'm no expert on Stoic philosophy, but at first the quote seems overly pessimistic. However, with context, you can see another perspective. If you expect the world to be perfect, you will quickly and consistently be disappointed. However, if you wake up expecting to deal with a lot of shit every day, you will be mentally prepared for it.

This is much like the expectation you need when you start out as an entrepreneur. By now you get how hard the journey is, but my goal has never been to dissuade you from taking the first step. Just the opposite—I want to *encourage* you to take that step.

The key is to have the right expectations from day one. Be prepared to bring your idea to a disinterested and skeptical world. Know from the start that it will be hard and require a lot of work. Enthusiasm helps you take the first step, but unrealistic expectations can be very dangerous. You risk becoming quickly disappointed with each and every setback.

Mr. Monkey will be there with you at the start and can often show up as unrealistic expectations—he'll act supportive, but he's really just screwing with you. The key is to talk to the monkey, listen to what he's saying about your dream, and see if his feedback is relevant. Then decide for sure if you really want to pursue your idea.

## NOTHING IS BIG FROM DAY ONE

Once you get going, the next step in expectation-setting is realizing that every really successful business started with a small idea that morphed into something much bigger over time.

When you read the story of Howard Schultz starting Starbucks, his goal was to recreate the café experience he'd had on a trip to Italy, and he started out with one shop in Seattle. Mark Zuckerberg started Facebook as a way to meet girls at Harvard. Even Jeff Bezos, who's extremely ambitious, had an initial tagline for Amazon that was "The World's Biggest Bookstore." Aggressive, but it didn't say "Become the next Walmart."

Every successful entrepreneurial journey starts with someone thinking, *There might be an opportunity here.* When you're choosing the opportunity you want to pursue, focus on which idea gives you the most energy. Research the market, but don't get concerned if the idea doesn't feel like it has the potential to be the next Facebook. Nothing does at the start.

Don't pick a business idea solely on profit potential either. Profitability is important, but it can't be your only motive. Septic tank maintenance is a profitable business with a big market, but will you feel passionate about emptying septic tanks every day? Sounds shitty to me (groan!) but if it works for you, then get after it.

The key is to focus on what you know and what you are passionate about, and then build a detailed plan from there. "Begin the begin," as R.E.M. sang back in the day.

Mr. Monkey will tell you not to do it. He'll tell you about all the things that can go wrong. He's an effective bastard.

The first step, as the old saying goes, is the hardest one. Do your research, make sure the idea is one that has potential and is something you will enjoy being associated with for a long time. Starting off with the right expectations will make the first step much easier. Taking that first steps leads to something called momentum. And momentum is a very real thing.

## SOMEDAY NEVER COMES

A few years into my entrepreneurial journey things seemed to be going pretty well—not great yet but certainly better than the early dark days. Somewhere after hiring the coke addict but before losing our largest customer. The business was growing fast but nothing was getting any easier. Actually, the bigger we got, the more I was working, and the entire job seemed to keep getting harder and harder. It pissed me off because it didn't seem fair.

Mr. Monkey came into my office one day and dropped himself into the old chair across from my desk. *"Mike, this entrepreneur shit is still a bitch, isn't it?"* His tone was unusually soft and I found this disarming. *"You have worked really hard—it is okay to feel exhausted and burned out. You deserve a break."*

I began to feel sorry for myself and lost my motivation. I had assumed that once the company got to a certain size everything would get easier. But it was still a grind. It was like pushing a bigger rock up a steeper hill. Mr. Monkey stood up, gave me a small hug, and walked slowly out of my office. I suspect he had a sly smile on his face. He was messing with me once again, but his tactics were different and more devious. He was tempting me to fall into the trap of false expectations, and he damn near succeeded.

My phone rang. It was Bill Egan, one of my first backers and a long-time board member. Bill is like a combination of

Warren Buffett and the Farmer's Almanac—a great investor filled with funny stories and curated insights. I always liked hearing from Bill.

As usual, we discussed sports and life for a few minutes, but Bill could sense my mood and asked what was going on. Feeling down, I shared my perspective with Bill about "the grind" and my growing disillusionment with the job. I was expecting Bill to give me a pep talk about how easier days were just around the corner, but I got a very different response.

"You're living in a fantasy world, Mike. You're hoping something's going to happen to make things easier, and it's not. It never gets easier. It just gets different. Someday never comes."

There is an old, sad song by Creedence Clearwater Revival called "Someday Never Comes" about a little boy hoping his deadbeat dad will return someday. I hate that song, but I am sure the reference would be lost on Bill. Regardless, his message hit me like a bucket of ice cold water dumped on my head. It snapped me out of my pity party and reminded me of what the reality of being an entrepreneur is all about.

*Someday never comes....* So stop waiting—or hoping—for it.

Once I processed this and changed my expectations, it was liberating. I stopped waiting for the day when "everything was working" as I realized I was chasing the impossible. My expectations were wrong.

If you expect that at a certain point, being an entrepreneur will become easy, you're doing yourself a disservice. The trick is to think like a professional athlete. Work tirelessly at your craft and look forward to the new challenges. If you are the best tennis player in the world, do you expect the finals at Wimbledon to one day "get easier?" No way. You keep working, setting new goals, adjusting your expectations.

Like the captain of a ship in the ocean, you can either wish the waves would stop, or you can shift your mindset to expect the storms and calms as part of the journey. When the big waves come, you'll be ready for them; you'll be prepared. And when rare moments of sunshine and calm are on the horizon, you'll be more than ready to sit back, even just for a moment, and enjoy the view. You know the journey will end someday—even if you don't know exactly how.

## AUGUST 4, 2014

"You're fired."

Bruce Dunlevie, long-time board member at ServiceSource, didn't use those exact words, but the message was the same. Another uneventful Monday suddenly turned on its ear. (Shit, I hate Mondays.)

My memory of that moment is fuzzy, but I think what he actually said was, "Mike, it's time for you to go."

I do remember my exact response: "Actually, Bruce, I think that time is *long* overdue."

I told you this wasn't going to be the typical rags to riches business story, didn't I?

Effective immediately, I would no longer be CEO of Service-Source. I had started my entrepreneurial journey back in 2001, and now, thirteen years later, it was over in an instant. An activist had taken a large ownership position in our stock, forced his way onto our board, and was growing impatient with the lack of increase in the stock price. I was the fall guy in his turnaround plan.

Public companies have to disclose this type of change immediately, so a press release would go out the next day letting the world know of my fate. Plans were already in place for our CFO to be named as the interim CEO. Clearly, this had been in the works for some time and several people at the company knew about it way before I did.

It felt like that moment in a mob movie when the gangster walks to the back of a car and finds an empty trunk. He turns to see his best friend standing next to him, hiding something behind his back. "What's this all about?" he demands, right before the blunt object strikes him in the back of the head.

My entrepreneurial run exceeded my wildest dreams and I had achieved more than I could ever imagine. I had a great wife, four beautiful kids, two dogs, two houses, and health and abundance. I knew I should be filled with gratitude. But I also knew that the headline for ServiceSource the following day would say, "Management shakeup," which everyone knows is the code word for "Fired CEO."

I cried. I yelled. I smashed some glassware and got drunk as a billy goat. It was one of the worst days of my life. It was one of Mr. Monkey's best days ever. He damn near broke his arm patting himself on the back.

The only thing that softened the blow was that I really did believe it was time for me to go. I had told my board this for well over a year. My expectations for the journey had started out small and mildly ambitious. More than anything, I wanted to build something. To take a risk, create a company with a culture that mattered. To make the time spent in the work third of life mean something.

But by the end, I was exhausted with the job and suffering from burnout. I'd become wealthy, and had begun to feel the pull of entitlement going to my head. The reasons I'd wanted to do the job were lost. The purity was long gone. My self-awareness slowly and invisibly turned into self-importance. My motivation and drive diminished.

Being fired would sting like hell for a long time, but in my heart I knew my expectations had gotten skewed. I was no longer the best person for the job. I wish that moment had come with a little ceremony; perhaps a careful discussion over a nice dinner and a glass of wine, instead of the hammer to head and the empty trunk. But such is life. You can still love a movie even if you hate the ending. It turns out Mr. Monkey's theatrical vision is *not* exactly on par with Martin Scorsese.

## *EXPECT* **DEFINITION: TO CONSIDER PROBABLE OR CERTAIN**

By now, I hope you agree with me that most of the blogs or articles written about entrepreneurship are, quite simply, bullshit. "Ten simple steps to success" or "Dream big and follow your passion" don't even begin to tell the story. They may be fun to read but—as I stated up front—too much and you will feel sad and unfulfilled. There is just so much more to it. So it is with setting and managing your expectations— there is a lot to it.

From the start, it is critical to set your expectations appropriately. Know that it will be hard and that surprises will come at you right from the start. The worst expectation of all is to think that the world owes you anything. Expecting the world to meet you and your dream with anything more than callous indifference is downright foolish. Make sure you are excited about your idea and that your enthusiasm comes from within. The hardest part is to get started and take the first step. Balanced expectations are critical from day one.

As you move through your experience, resetting these expectations will help keep your feet planted on the ground as you continue to reach for the stars. It will also enable you to stay present and focus on what matters in the moment. If you pine for the future—someday—you will miss the present moments that really matter. You will miss the small victories that happen every day.

As you make progress, it will be easy to lose perspective and forget what matters. If your expectations get too large, you might think you don't have to keep up with all the hard work that got you ahead in the first place. That is how you end up in the back of a trunk, your head bleeding, wondering how it all went wrong...

In the end, the most important thing will be that you gave it a try. Of course, you want to build something great and meaningful—that desire is so important. But even with the undesirable end to my entrepreneurial movie, I would do it all over again. The end really doesn't matter; it is indeed all about the journey. Theodore Roosevelt's speech "The Man in the Arena" says it all:

> *It is not the critic who counts; not the man who points out how the strong man stumbles, or where the doer of deeds could have done them better. The credit belongs to the man who is actually in the arena, whose face is marred by dust and sweat and blood... who at the best knows in the end the triumph of high achievement, and who at the worst, if he fails, at least fails while daring greatly, so that his place shall never be with those cold and timid souls who neither know victory nor defeat.*

## ONWARD!

The journey of a thousand miles does, in fact, begin with the first step. Entrepreneurship is going to be a long journey, but if you spend too much time thinking about it, you will never start out. Set your expectations and take that first step. Then keep walking. It *will* be worth it. Here are few final tips to help you manage your expectations throughout your journey. And keep reminding yourself: it *is* all about the journey, not the destination.

## MONKEY MINDERS #5: HOW TO
## MANAGE EXPECTATIONS

- *Let someone talk you out of it.* Whenever someone I know is thinking of starting a business I recommend this bizarre idea. Go to someone you really respect, tell them your idea and beg them to talk you out of starting the business. Listen to all the reasons why your idea is dumb or why the business will fail and see how it changes your conviction level. If you start to waiver or the person succeeds in talking you out of it, that is probably a good thing—you just saved several years of pain. If no one can you talk you out of your idea, then you might just be on to something. Or you might be crazy—but you have to be more than a little crazy to be an entrepreneur. This is a good test for your mental readiness to start the journey.

- *Next five years test.* At Next Coast ventures, we ask all aspiring entrepreneurs one simple question: "In five years, if everything goes just okay, will you be happy or sad that you started this business? Will you be passionate about the subject matter even if it isn't a great success?" We see so many entrepreneurs who have a pretty good idea, but we can tell that deep down they aren't passionate about the business. This is a very real warning sign. The ups and downs of building a business, regardless of size, are all-consuming. That needs to be your clear expectation. This test will help you measure your commitment to the idea without wearing rose-colored glasses.

- *Make short-term goals.* Set a big vision for what you want to achieve, but quickly break down the five things you need to do in the next day, the next week, or the next month. The journey has to start with one small step. It's motivating to imagine what the view will be at the top of the mountain, but get your expectations in line and focus on getting started. Then keep walking. Take the small tactical steps to start the climb.

Remember that there are no get-rich-quick schemes. There are only get-rich-slow schemes. It takes blood, sweat, and tears. Accept that and just get started. Start walking.

- *100 percent rule.* Michael Jordan, the greatest NBA player of all time, said, "You miss 100 percent of the shots you don't take." I apply the same concept to business with this simple statement: "100 percent of the businesses that don't get started fail." Think about it; if you see an opportunity, it's pretty likely that someone, somewhere is going to take a risk and turn that dream into a reality. Yes, it's risky, but so is crossing the street. After all, your crazy idea might just work. *Somebody* is going to make it happen. Why shouldn't it be you?

# CONCLUSION

## MY LIFELONG FRENEMY, MR. MONKEY

*"Twenty years from now, you will be more disappointed by the things you didn't do than by the ones you did do. So throw off the bowlines. Sail away from the safe harbor. Catch the trade winds in your sail. Explore. Dream. Discover."*

—SARAH FRANCES BROWN

Today, I have a clear and firm expectation: I am going to finish writing this damn book.

I'm sitting in my guest house at our family vacation home in Jackson, Wyoming. The views surrounding the property are stunning. There is no smell of oil being refined; Toledo, Ohio, is far away from here, literally and figuratively. The couch is comfortable and the room is filled with photographs of my family and friends. I can hear my four children playing outside, and my two dogs are lounging on the floor near my feet.

I've accomplished more than I would have ever thought possible back in my early days in Toledo. I've done it through hard work, dedication, and a shit ton of luck. But for a few lucky breaks, I know that right now, I could be finishing up a long shift at the Jeep plant, ready to head out to the bar for a shot and a beer, with plans of drinking my frustrations away. Or locked down in a maximum security prison, cursing myself for the careless handling of my murder weapon of choice.

It's a good life. I can imagine my mom, grandma, and Uncle Joe sitting together up in heaven saying, "It must be nice." That image makes me smile. All I can say is, "Well, yes...yes... it *is* nice!" I am a lucky bastard.

*But that's not what this book was about.*

Sitting down to work, I hit play on Florence and the Machine's *The Odyssey*, pop in my earbuds, and open my laptop. I've got a big cup of coffee. I've blocked off my calendar. It's time to finish this damn thing. I'm typing the final section and feeling like the finish line is in sight.

Then I hear him.

His voice is, as always, unmistakable.

*"Why are you doing this, Mike? No one's going to read this book."*

Mr. Monkey's here. Just like always.

"I run a venture capital firm. I worked in Silicon Valley for twenty years. I bought a company and took it public," I tell him. "I think I have some useful information to share."

Mr. Monkey grins at me, and takes a sip of my coffee, slobbering all over the mug. He's middle-aged now. He's put on a few pounds, and he's not as muscular as he used to be. He's got some gray hair around his temples. I've got some gray hairs, too. We're fifty now, my monkey and me.

*"What are you doing, Mike?"* Mr. Monkey says, dragging a chair over to sit next to me at the computer. *"Yeah, you've had some luck but you haven't been that successful. Smerklo isn't exactly a household name. You've made some money but nowhere near as much as those really successful entrepreneurs."*

I let his comments slide, focus on the paragraph I'm trying to write, and begin to type a few more words on the page. He hates to be ignored, old Mr. Monkey, and so he turns up the heat one more notch and gets personal.

*"Sure, your company went public, but have you checked the stock price of ServiceSource lately?"* He's on a roll, and he utters his death blow. *"I can't recall how that movie ended for you. Hmm, let me see...didn't you get fired? What does SHAPE stand for again?"*

Son of a bitch still knows what buttons to push. Even after all these years, the bastard never wastes time or beats around the bush. He's as subtle as a kick in the private parts.

"I did fine," I say, gesturing to the mountain view out the window, snow just starting to fall on the trees off in the distance.

The monkey shrugs. *"Your story is kind of interesting, but who really gives a damn? Is anybody going to read this? Personally, I would rather read that blog about what Jeff Bezos eats for breakfast."*

I know better than to listen to him, but then I hear my phone buzzing. I look down; it's a text message from a friend. I pick up my phone and quickly send a response. Fifteen minutes pass, and I'm still checking stock prices and looking through headlines on CNN.

When I look over, that monkey is smiling, because he won once again.

The bastard seems to have changed his game as I have gotten older. He doesn't scream and yell much anymore; that's far too obvious, and not as effective as it used to be. He draws from a different list of failures, and his many voices seem to have changed as well. But his goal remains the same. As always, he is a powerful, brilliant, manipulative motherfucker, and he's still very good at his job.

In the same way that I realized that the roller coaster of entrepreneurship never ends, I also understand now that no level of success will ever make Mr. Monkey go away.

I hope this book has helped you start to recognize the monkey that follows you around. He's your frenemy for life, and he'll keep changing his voices throughout your journey. Start to listen a bit closer and you will recognize the voice. Teacher, coach, parent, friend, partner—it really doesn't matter. The key is starting to listen.

Sometimes, Mr. Monkey will be so loud you can't avoid him. But most of the time, he's a little whisper that you are not quite sure you've heard. The specifics of his message change as you do, but he's always there.

By now, you've heard all my stories—at least those that are fit for print—about my struggles with the hairy beast. I tried desperately to make him go away, but nothing ever worked. Finally, after fifty years, I now seem him for what he is.

That doesn't mean I've mastered Mr. Monkey. That would be impossible. I also don't expect him to leave me alone anymore, but that is okay.

And *that* is what this book is about.

Mr. Monkey isn't going away for you either, but he doesn't deserve the credit for preventing you from going after your dreams. The goal of this book is to give you the tools to work *with* him instead of against him. To respond to him instead of overreacting or giving in. Invite him in for a chat, pour him his own coffee, and hear what he has to say. Listen to him, but see him for what he is—and what he isn't.

That is what the SHAPE formula is meant to help you do: master the mental part of entrepreneurship. The SHAPE formula was developed so that each letter can stand on its own. But like a pyramid, the real power comes when you build upon the previous concept. **S**elf-awareness helps you be objective about your strengths and weaknesses. This in turn shows you where you need to get **H**elp. Advice and input from others will enable your **A**uthentic voice to emerge. Feeling comfortable in your own skin helps you remain **P**ersistent. Persistence and long-term thinking keep your **E**xpectations in check throughout your journey.

Mr. Monkey will be there the whole way. The goal is to use him to your advantage. Like a great competitor in the chess game of life, Mr. Monkey can push you to sharpen your game. He's never going away, so learn to make the best of your "partnership."

*"So, you're never going to write this book, Mike, are you?"* Mr. Monkey says.

Annie, my black lab, brings me a rope bone, gently nudging it into my hand, hoping for a game of tug. Old Miracle entered heaven's gates a few years ago, and Annie has slowly taken on his role in giving me unconditional love and support. She wags her tail expectantly, looking up at me with her big, adoring eyes.

"Why can't you be more like Annie?" I say to Mr. Monkey.

*"Just be happy I'm housebroken,"* Mr. Monkey says, wagging his tail like Annie.

"Go take a nap, dude," I say. "I know you don't think I'll finish this book, but your subtle reminders are—like always—motivating me to get after it. Thanks for the push, jackass...."

Mr. Monkey sighs and rests his head on his knees. I turn the music back on, pick up my laptop and start to type.

## NOW IT'S YOUR TURN

The world needs you to raise your hand now more than ever.

I know you can do it, and I hope this book helps you take your first step or continue on your journey. Your dreams, your ideas, your vision—they really do matter. Big or small, building something will make a difference and there has never been a better time than now. Real change in the world will only come from the crazy entrepreneurs that forge ahead, develop a clear vision, and then work tirelessly to turn the dream into a reality.

As Nelson Mandela said, "It always seems impossible until it is done."

The world needs the benefits of your ideas. It doesn't matter how big your dream stretches. You have the opportunity to enrich the lives of your customers, your employees, your community, and possibly help the world at large. Don't hold yourself back.

Remember, you are going to spend a third of your life working. Do you really want to spend your precious time helping someone else reach their dream? That's okay for some, but if you feel the urge to break out, then I hope this book helps you get after it.

The first step is the hardest, but taking that step puts you in the small class of humans who took the step. The "work third" part of your life will mean something, regardless of the outcome. You went out, and you got into the arena, and you took the plunge. You are going to find the best (and worst) in yourself and others. But at least you're *in* the arena while others are whittling away their precious time watching from some bland corporate cubicle.

The SHAPE formula is just one of many tools you will need to be successful as an entrepreneur. I hope it helps you as you pursue your dreams. We all have our Mr. or Mrs. Monkey to tell us we can't do it. That's normal, and it is okay. It won't be easy or simple, but nothing worth pursuing is supposed to be.

The future is at hand, and what that looks like is entirely up to you. If a poor kid from Toledo, Ohio, like me can follow the entrepreneurial path, I am pretty sure you can do it as well. Trust me when I say that there is not a better job in the world.

Now is your time.

Get out of the shower, dry off, put some clothes on, and get going. Start your journey. Take the first step. Keep after it. The journey is going to be worth it.

Oh, and, for me: please tell Mr. Monkey to *fuck off*.

Now make it happen!

# ACKNOWLEDGMENTS

*The only thing that can change where you are now to where you will be in five years from now are the books you read, the people you meet, and the dreams you dream.*

—LOU HOLTZ, FOOTBALL COACH

I heard the above quote on a scratchy audio recording of a speech Lou Holtz made in the late 1980s. I was in high school at the time, and I took his recommendation to heart. The books I've read have shaped every part of my life. The dreams I've chased have helped me achieve more than I ever thought possible. But most impactful of all, it has been the people I've met over my journey who have made all the difference. So many people have helped me, coached me, influenced me, and encouraged me that it is impossible for me to list them comprehensively.

They all show up in this book one way or another. Several

individuals from my professional life have been called out by name in this book, and I hope they don't mind that I did so. I also hope I got the facts somewhat right. Memory is a son of a bitch, as they say, and my lack of attention to detail has been sufficiently noted. I know I've probably missed several names that should have been part of this story, and for that I apologize.

First and foremost, I want to thank my wife Abby and my four children—Rhett, Roark, Rylan, and River—for all the support and humor they provided me while I wrote this book. The book was written primarily during family time—late nights, early mornings, and weekends—but they encouraged me to keep after it and finish it. Abby has been with me through all of the amazing highs and faith-crushing lows of entrepreneurship, and has supported me through it all; I love her more than words can express. My four children have always been my biggest fans, and I hope they are proud of my work. Roark, thank you for your endless curiosity. Rylan, thank you for challenging me to keep after it. Rhett, thank you for your creativity—and thanks for designing the book cover for me. River, your smile and enthusiasm make my world. I love you all and am filled with gratitude for my greatest blessing: the Smerklo six!

To the team at Next Coast Ventures, in particular my business partner Tom Ball: thanks for letting me get away from my "day job" to get this book done. For all those who were part of the ServiceSource journey: thank you for all the sacrifice, hard work, and dedication as we tried to make a boring company into one that would be memorable. It's your call on whether your "work third" mattered, but I know in my heart that we built something special. Thank you to each and every 'Sourcer. Keep winning as a team wherever your journey takes you.

Thank you to my YPO chaptermates, and in particular my forum, for encouraging me to "get after it and write the damn book!" I needed the push.

Thank you to all my mentors—too numerous to count—who helped me throughout my journey. This book represents all your voices coming together as one. The SHAPE formula is a compilation of concepts that you taught me. This story is really your story—thank you!

Writing this book has been a lot like starting out as an entrepreneur—if I knew how hard it was going to be I probably would have never undertaken it in the first place. In that regard, I owe a great deal of thanks to the entire team at Scribe Media. Thank you for your coaching, editing, and patience with all the ups and downs that go with writing a book.

To my scattered family from Toledo and beyond: thank you. It was all done with love in mind; of that, I was always certain.

My description of getting "out" was mental, not geographical. You provided the foundation for much of my lifelong learning and development. To my sister Liz, I owe a lifelong debt of gratitude for always helping me make sense of Mr. Monkey and all his various voices. Most of all, I send a prayer of thanks to my mother in heaven. She always believed in me, encouraged me, and pushed me to do more every step of the way.

Finally, to all the entrepreneurs in the world: I salute you. The courage, commitment, dedication—and insanity—it takes to step into the arena and try to turn a dream into a reality is known only to a select few. Feel proud. You are in the arena, fighting hard, and giving it your all. Your dedication, hard work, passion, and commitment are my truest inspiration. Thank you for all that you do day in and day out. Keep battling that monkey—and keep on making it happen!

# ABOUT THE AUTHOR

**MIKE SMERKLO** is an experienced entrepreneur, investor, and business leader driven by the desire to turn ideas into reality. Having bought and scaled a small business into a publicly traded company worth nearly a billion dollars in value, he has a deep understanding of the hard work, dedication, and grit that truly powers successful entrepreneurship. Today, as the co-founder and managing director of Next Coast Ventures, Smerklo is a champion for a new generation of entrepreneurs building disruptive companies in big markets.

Smerklo grew up in a blue-collar family outside of Toledo, Ohio, with dreams of achieving something *more* with his life. After working his way through college to earn an accounting degree and moving to Chicago to launch his CPA career, he eventually talked his way into a junior analyst gig with the Wall Street investment bank Lehman Brothers. While he hated the job, surviving two years of hellish 100-hour workweeks and countless spreadsheets (*so many spreadsheets*) gave Smerklo a solid understanding of finance and company building. He went on to earn an MBA from the Kellogg School of Management at Northwestern University and experienced the Silicon Valley dot-com boom as an investment banker at Morgan Stanley.

Smerklo was recruited by legendary entrepreneurs Marc Andreessen and Ben Horowitz as one of the first employees of their new startup, LoudCloud. Here, he learned from the very best about what it takes to grow a company from an idea to and beyond an initial public offering. Smerklo began his own entrepreneurial journey in 2003, purchasing ServiceSource, a thirty-person technology services startup in San Francisco. As CEO over the next twelve years, he grew the business into a successful 3,000-person publicly traded company with close to $300 million in revenue.

He has developed a new perspective on entrepreneurship at the helm of the Austin-based firm Next Coast Ventures, which has backed more than forty companies across two funds to help startup founders achieve their goals. Mike and his wife spend the bulk of their free time chasing their four children. Visit www.mikesmerklo.com to read his blog and learn more.

Made in the USA
Coppell, TX
07 November 2020

40935488R00111